PUNCH NEEDLE
RUG HOOKING
HANDBOOK

techniques & playful projects

CRYSTAL ROSS

stashBOOKS
an imprint of C&T Publishing

Text and instructional photography copyright © 2025 by Crystal Ross

Artwork and lifestyle photography copyright © 2025 by C&T Publishing, Inc.

PUBLISHER: Amy Barrett-Daffin

CREATIVE DIRECTOR: Gailen Runge

SENIOR EDITOR: Roxane Cerda

EDITOR: Madison Moore

ASSOCIATE EDITOR: Karly Wallace

TECHNICAL EDITOR: Linda Johnson

COPY EDITOR: Emily King

COVER/BOOK DESIGNER: April Mostek

PRODUCTION COORDINATOR: Tim Manibusan

ILLUSTRATOR: Aliza Shalit

PHOTOGRAPHY COORDINATOR: Rachel Ackley

FRONT COVER PHOTOGRAPHY by Crystal Ross

SUBJECTS AND INSTRUCTIONAL PHOTOGRAPHY by Crystal Ross

LIFESTYLE PHOTOGRAPHY by Chelle Wooten and Crystal Ross

Published by Stash Books, an imprint of C&T Publishing, Inc., P.O. Box 1456, Lafayette, CA 94549

Attention Teachers: C&T Publishing, Inc., encourages the use of our books as texts for teaching. You can find lesson plans for many of our titles at ctpub.com or contact us at ctinfo@ctpub.com.

We take great care to ensure that the information included in our products is accurate and presented in good faith, but no warranty is provided, nor are results guaranteed. Having no control over the choices of materials or procedures used, neither the author nor C&T Publishing, Inc., shall have any liability to any person or entity with respect to any loss or damage caused directly or indirectly by the information contained in this book. For your convenience, we post an up-to-date listing of corrections on our website (ctpub.com). If a correction is not already noted, please contact our customer service department at ctinfo@ctpub.com or P.O. Box 1456, Lafayette, CA 94549.

Trademark (™) and registered trademark (®) names are used throughout this book. Rather than use the symbols with every occurrence of a trademark or registered trademark name, we are using the names only in the editorial fashion and to the benefit of the owner, with no intention of infringement.

Library of Congress Cataloging-in-Publication Data

Names: Ross, Crystal Marie, 1982- author.

Title: Punch needle rug hooking handbook : techniques & playful projects / Crystal Ross.

Description: Lafayette, CA : Stash Books, [2025] | Summary: "In this handbook, learn everything you need to know to punch needle rug hook, from beginner techniques to expert tips. Explore fifteen cozy, folk-inspired masterpieces with designs that feature a tapestry of floral, animal, and patterned motifs. You'll learn the elements of design and inspiration for crafting unique punch needle creations"-- Provided by publisher.

Identifiers: LCCN 2024037583 | ISBN 9781644034866 (trade paperback) | ISBN 9781644034873 (ebook)

Subjects: LCSH: Rugs, Hooked.

Classification: LCC TT850 .R677 2025 | DDC 746.7/4--dc23/eng/20241008

LC record available at https://lccn.loc.gov/2024037583

Printed in China

10 9 8 7 6 5 4 3 2 1

DEDICATION

To Velma and Jordan: You are my home and creative fuel.

ACKNOWLEDGMENTS

Special thanks to my parents, my brother, and to Madison Moore, for her kind encouragement and work on this book.

CONTENTS

INTRODUCTION

There's excitement bubbling up around the subject of punch needle. It's a craft with a long history, though it has somehow eluded popular attention for several generations. Now, in recent years, it has crept (or really, flown) back into the spotlight.

The official name for the craft featured in this book is *punch needle rug hooking*, and is closely related to traditional rug hooking. But it features a unique tool and technique. I mention this because I grew up surrounded by the traditional type, and it's had an effect on my approach and appreciation for the medium.

From an early age, my environment instilled an appreciation for hooked rugs. My home province of Nova Scotia has a rich history in the craft; my mother is from Chéticamp, NS, a small French Acadian village once known as the rug hooking capital of the world, and my father is from Pictou County, NS, where the rug hooking company, Garrett's—by far the largest producer of rug hooking patterns for 80 years—was headquartered. Hooked rugs were always displayed on the walls of our home when I was growing up. Carefully preserved under glass and displayed in frames, they were too good for the floor! These were more than just decor; they were sentimental pieces that represented our family. Even the hooked coasters on our tables were there to be admired, never used (although we *might* have tossed them around like flying discs when we were kids).

This love for the craft isn't unique to our family, especially here on the east coast of Canada where rug hooking is embedded in our craft culture. Many families throughout the North American Eastern Seaboard share these generational connections too, with fond memories of their parents, grandparents, and great-grandparents crafting rugs. My maternal grandparents were exceptional rug hookers, and whenever we'd visit, there would almost always be a rug hooking frame set up in the living room with a beautiful work in progress.

Still, it wasn't until 2017 when I found my own passion for rug making, after textile artist Arounna Khounnoraj (@bookhou) sparked a frenzy using something called an *Oxford Punch Needle*—a tool that produced hooked rugs with ease and efficiency. The images of her gorgeous pieces spread like wildfire, and for me, they were a sign that I could take the medium in my own direction. (Arounna Khounnoraj is also a C&T author, and you should check out her title, *Contemporary Patchwork*.)

Much of the resurgence of punch needle can be traced back to the Oxford Punch Needle, a tool created by Amy Oxford, who is herself a great teacher and preservationist of the craft. This brand of needle has become one of the most popular tools for its ease and quality, and is my go-to for making rugs.

Today we are witnessing a fresh take on this storied category of fiber art. And how wonderful that it has deep roots and heaps of long-standing knowledge to accompany it!

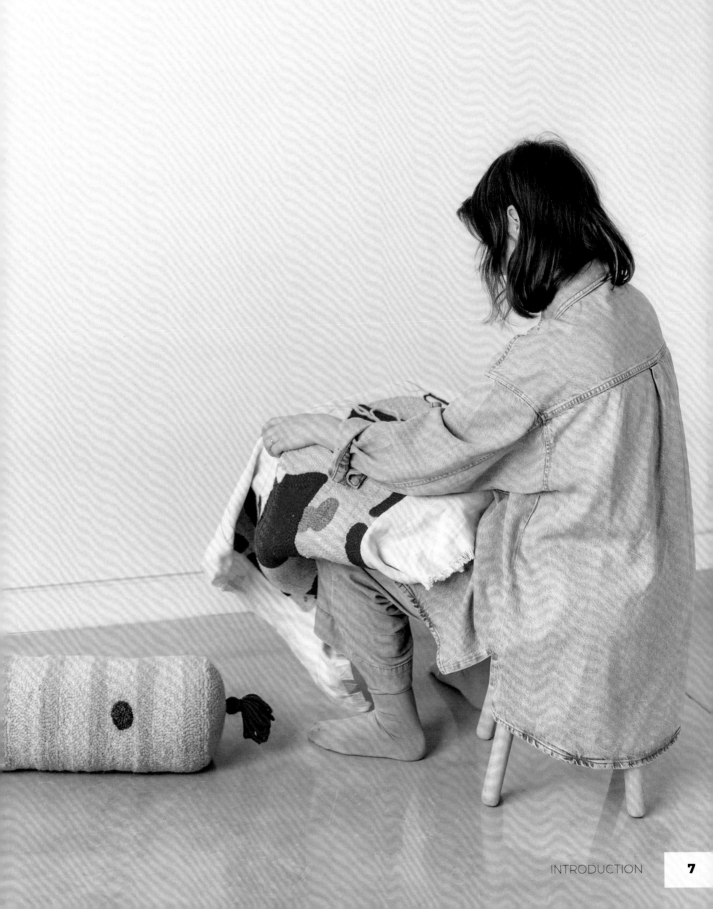

I've written this book to share my enthusiasm and to encourage you to dive into the craft, too—the benefits are many. Punch needle is the perfect craft to accompany you whether you are on the couch or in your studio. With just a few tools and some simple instructions, you'll be equipped with everything you need to get started. I have found punch needle rug hooking to be a simple and creatively limitless form of making with very few rules or boundaries—with a punch needle in hand, you're free to draw any subject and color outside any line, much like the freedom experienced through painting.

Added bonus? In addition to adorning your walls and floors, your finished textile objects can serve many different functions and be sewn into an endless list of three-dimensional shapes.

Whether or not you've already tested the waters with a punch needle, if you want to learn how to craft sturdy, functional pieces (even full-size durable rugs!), this is the right place for you. Regardless of where you are on your rug-making adventure, I know you'll find this handbook useful in providing all you need to propel your crafting journey forward!

Working on a Chéticamp frame (see Looking Back, page 11)

What a happy and useful way to express your creative talents—just as grandmother did—through a quaint, but ever new craft.

What keener satisfaction can anyone have than that which is derived from creating with your own hands something beautiful ... practical ... useful. Something which will be a source of pleasure and satisfaction for you and yours for years to come."

EXCERPT FROM A GARRETT'S BLUENOSE PATTERN CATALOG. Nanette Ryan and Doreen Wright, Garretts and the Bluenose Rugs of Nova Scotia. Mahone Bay, NS. Reprinted by Spruce Top Rug Hooking Studio, 1995.

A BIT OF TEXTILE HISTORY

As you dive into this new wave of punch needle, I want to start by sharing some context about the craft and its history. Though an embroidery hoop is a popular way of displaying punch needling online, none of the projects in this book are made or displayed that way. I'm encouraging you to explore the world of punch needle *outside* the embroidery hoop. We're drawing from a history of making large, functional items.

WHAT IS PUNCH NEEDLE RUG HOOKING?

Punch needle rug hooking is a specific technique used for crafting rugs that descends from a North American tradition of rug hooking. Punch hooked rugs (often called punched rugs and, confusingly, sometimes called hooked rugs) are meant for a wide range of uses, both functional and decorative. The punch needle rug hooking technique is different from rug hooking. First, you stretch a woven backing taut over a frame. Then you use a punch needle to push yarn *down* into the backing. The side facing you is called the *stitch side*, and is (usually) the back of the work when displayed. This process forms loops of yarn held tightly within the weave of the backing fabric. These loops, called the *pile*, appear on the front of the rug. The choice of which side to display is usually a matter of personal preference, but for functional floor rugs, the pile side should face up.

Demonstrating an early punch needle called a **Bluenose Rug Hooker**
Provided by the Rug Hooking Museum of North America

Rug hooking (also known as traditional rug hooking) shares many similarities to punch needle rug hooking, but with rug hooking, yarn or strips of material are pulled *up* through the woven backing using a tool called a *hook*. The pile side (the front side when displayed) of the rug is also the working side, so it faces you as you hook. The back side of a rug hooked piece is rarely shown.

Other punch needle crafts share many similarities with punch needle rug hooking, but they are usually meant for decorative purposes only. These other crafts include miniature punch needle (also called Russian punch needle), embroidery punch needle, and Japanese *bunka shishu*. Generally, each of these styles of punch needle use specific tools sized for fine yarn or thread that is much smaller than the yarn used for punch needle rug hooking.

Rug tufting is yet another popular form of rug making, one that has earned a lot of attention on social media. It involves using a handheld (electric or pneumatic) tufting gun that pushes yarn through fabric on what is usually a large upright frame. The machine automates the process of creating a loop or cut pile, and works at very high speeds. While tufting artists do need to take the extra step of gluing and backing their rugs with a separate fabric, these guns definitely save time and increase production levels, especially when compared to the length of time it takes to create hand-hooked or punched rugs. Tufting guns have provided great opportunity for small-scale producers and artisans to earn a living from crafting rugs.

For more on the differences between the tools used in these various crafts, see Tools and Materials (page 14).

LOOKING BACK

Historians believe that traditional rug hooking, the precursor to punch needle rug hooking, originated in the early to mid-nineteenth century. This North American folk art is said to have started from the desire to beautify and bring comfort to the home. According to Mildred Cole Péladeau in *Rug Hooking in Maine 1838–1940*, the craft grew through "friendly competition among neighbors," who, when wanting to impress one another, made decorations for the hearth—the central gathering place of the home. It's likely that these makers started with shirred or yarn-sewn rugs for the hearth, before eventually developing a new and sturdier form of rug making: rug hooking.

Woman with display of hooked rugs
Nova Scotia Archives, W. R. MacAskill, accession no. 1987-453 no 2653

These early hooked rugs were made by resourceful women of humble means who drew their own patterns and used whatever was available to craft their rugs. A bent nail was often used as a hook; a burlap sack was stretched for the backing; strips of spent clothing were used to form the loops. They transformed these plain and ordinary materials into functional works of art, bringing creativity and comfort into their everyday lives.

As rug hooking grew throughout eastern parts of Canada and along the American Eastern Seaboard, it rooted itself as an important domestic and artistic pursuit among women. Artisans honed their skills through the later part of the nineteenth century, refining their techniques and materials. The craft began to change rapidly in the last decades of the 1800s, as preprinted patterns became available and desirable. New tools were being developed too, and in 1881, a machinist from Ohio named Ebenezer Ross patented the very first punch needle rug hooking tool.

Ross's earliest needles were somewhat cumbersome devices, meant to mechanize and speed up the rug hooking process. He made many variations on his first tool, and over the years, others followed his lead, hoping to simplify and improve upon his original design with the goal of automating more of the rug hooking process.

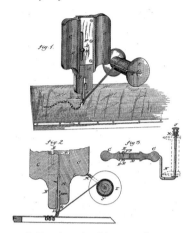

E. Ross's embroidery machine, patented 1881

The advent of these speedy, handheld punch needle tools coincided with the influential philosophies of the Arts and Crafts Movement, a movement that valued quality handmade wares over factory-made ones. This transformed the rug hooking industry and the spirit behind it. What once was a domestic art form became an entrepreneurial endeavor, for both men and women. There was lots of demand for handmade home textiles.

Hooking famous Cheticamp Rug
Nova Scotia Archives, Nova Scotia Information Service, no. 13107

Some makers switched to punch needles for speed, while others held on to their trusty hooks. But no matter the tool, the industry grew, and was unfortunately marked by long hours and poor wages for the artisans. At the same time, the demand brought work and money to many rural communities, raising the standard of living for many people. This influx of work also led to the development of culturally significant rugs that were unique to the region where they were made.

In the early twentieth century, styles, methods of production, and materials varied by area, but the popularity of hooked rugs, both punched and traditionally hooked, soared. This is especially true of the rugs made in the rural French Acadian community of Chéticamp, Nova Scotia. Traditional rug hookers, under the design guidance of American artist Lillian Burke, created rugs that became status symbols for the wealthy and were highly sought-after for their fine craftsmanship. These rugs were made in the prevailing style of the time and featured a wide range of motifs, including floral sprays, nature scenes, and other elements often inspired by historic textiles. Many of these rugs were custom-made for Ms. Burke's discerning clients, including a notable piece known as the "Chéticamp Savonnerie Carpet," completed in 1937. This particular rug was a monumental task, with eight women working on it for over six months, resulting in a finished piece measuring 648 square feet. It is believed by many to be the largest hand-hooked rug ever created. Even today, Chéticamp rugs are recognized as a form of fine art unique to the region, and are proudly displayed on walls rather than used as floor coverings.

Lillian Burke, her rug hookers, and their giant rug
Attribution: Nancy Korber, Librarian/Archivist, Fairchild Tropical Botanic Garden from the collection of photographer Dr. David Fairchild

The arrival of industrial rug-making processes, most notably the tufting gun, contributed to the demise of many small rug-making collectives. By the 1950s, their numbers had significantly declined.

While the popularity of rug hooking has fluctuated through recent generations, the tradition has been fairly well preserved, and has always found artisans to approach it as a hobby, craft, and art form. Punch needle rug hooking, on the other hand, lost much of its earlier traction over time. But now that it has found popularity on a mainstream level, the momentum of rug making has taken off once again. A burgeoning industry has emerged, offering user-friendly punch needles, a growing community of artists dedicated to the craft, and renewed interest in handmade home goods. I hope you can see yourself as a part of this history too—with so much to be inspired by, there's always room for new artists. I can't wait to see what you make as a part of this beautiful tradition!

Connecting with the Craft

Like I mentioned in the introduction, my connection to rug hooking is a personal one. My grandparents, Gérard and Annie-Rose Deveau, were notable actors in preserving this craft's history and were the driving force behind establishing the Élizabeth LeFort Gallery in Chéticamp, Nova Scotia. LeFort was one of rug hooking's most renowned artists, known for her stunning textile portraits.

My grandmother also spent years researching the history of rug making in Chéticamp, culminating in the book, *The History of Chéticamp Hooked Rugs and Their Artisans*. They were also both talented rug hooking artists in their own right, and inspired many, including myself, to take up the craft. Several of their pieces can be found on display in the rug hooking gallery at *Les Trois Pignons* cultural center in Chéticamp, Nova Scotia.

TOOLS AND MATERIALS

With the speedy growth in popularity of crafts like punch needle, rug hooking, tufting, and more, there are lots of related rug-making tools on the market. It can be hard to sort through all the terminology and nail down exactly what's needed for punch needle rug hooking. If you're feeling confused, this guide will help simplify your search for the perfect setup!

This chapter breaks down what each tool and material is used for, highlighting what works best and what won't suit our purposes.

PUNCH NEEDLE RUG HOOKING TOOLS

Our craft is called *punch needle rug hooking*. Though it's similar to traditional rug hooking, it's still a unique form. For more about the distinctions between these crafts, see What Is Punch Needle Rug Hooking? (page 10).

When purchasing a punch needle, there are two size-related elements to pay attention to. The first is the needle's yarn capacity. The needle can be suited for bulky or thin yarn. The second is the needle's length. The needle length affects the size of the loops created as you punch.

Oxford Punch Needles

The Oxford Punch Needle is the gold standard for this craft, and is, in large part, the reason why punch needle rug hooking has grown so much in popularity in recent years. Why is it so great? It's simple to use and a cinch to thread. Simply thread the yarn through the eye of the needle, and pull it into the slot in the handle. Yarn glides through the needle without catching or snagging. Its smooth and sturdy construction is reliable and built to last. And, very importantly, the ergonomic handle is comfortable to hold over extended periods of time.

One perceived limitation of this tool is that it is not adjustable. Oxford Punch Needles are sold in a variety of fixed needle lengths. But I find this can also be an advantage when working on a large project. Adjustable tools are not always as reliable, and when used over extended periods of time, they may slip out of position while punching. This is never an issue with the Oxford Punch Needle.

Oxford Punch Needles are sold in *regular* and *fine* sizes (which refer to the weight of yarn they accommodate) and in different needle lengths that create a variety of loop heights. The Oxford regular size 10 is a great all-purpose tool to start with. It works beautifully using bulky yarns, and creates a perfect ¼″ loop. It's the tool I've used to craft every project in this book.

Unbranded Punch Needles (Oxford-Style)

There are lots of punch needles on the market that look nearly identical to their authentic Oxford counterparts. But many of these tools are made cheaply and come with frustrating barriers. With cheap production come defects like metal burrs and unsanded wooden cores that can catch and snag at yarn. Their needles are usually made from thin materials that don't keep their shape over time and are inconsistently sized. The handles are also more likely to split. Buyer beware! I definitely recommend investing in an Oxford Punch Needle from the beginning.

Lavor Punch Needles

This European-made and economic punch needle is a great, reliable, and easy-to-use option. It comes in a variety of sizes for different yarns, but the 5.5mm (also known as *chunky* or XL needle) option is great for the bulky-yarn projects in this book. The needle length is adjustable and can punch seven different loop heights.

Its construction is very solid. The handle made from recycled plastic is arguably not quite as comfortable as the Oxford, but this might be a matter of personal preference.

The Lavor needs to be threaded using a thin wire needle threader. This is easy to do, but it can become a chore when repeatedly doing so for a large piece. There is also a little more room for error when working with an adjustable needle, since, as I mentioned earlier, the needle can sometimes slip out of place. Overall, the Lavor is an excellent choice with a lot of creative flexibility wrapped up in a single tool.

If you want to punch a ¼″ loop, like you'll need to for the projects in this book, choose the second-lowest setting on the needle, with four notches visible above the handle.

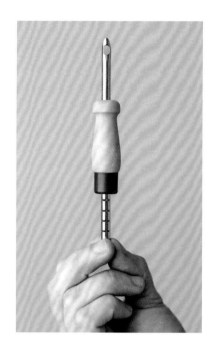

Craftsman's Punch Needle

The Craftsman's punch needle is a great vintage tool with a lot of options. It threads like the Oxford, and the needle length is adjustable like the Lavor. Unfortunately, I find the handle can be uncomfortable to hold over long periods, and it is a difficult needle to find in today's market. It comes in several sizes, so for our purposes, if you're using a version of this option, make sure it can produce a ¼″ loop and can accommodate a bulky weight yarn.

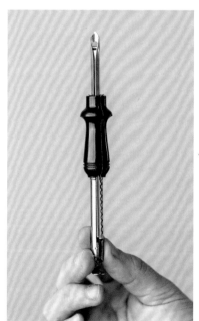

Tube-Style Punch Needles

Tube-style punch needles have a fixed needle length. They're an inexpensive entry point, and quality varies by brand. Generally, these needles are a good value if you're looking to test your interest in the craft. They also need to be threaded using a wire needle threader. Remember that for the projects in this book, you need to purchase one meant for bulky yarn.

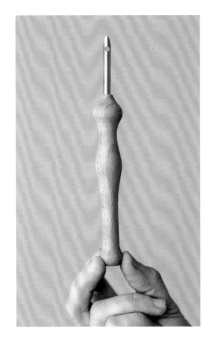

Traditional Rug Hooks

You'll remember from Looking Back (page 11) that punch needle rug hooking was born out of traditional rug hooking. So will a traditional rug hook work for this craft? Yes … and no. You can create the projects in this book with a rug hook, but the process will be different.

A traditional rug hook can produce a similar loop, but the technique is opposite from a punch needle. With a rug hook, you pull loops up (toward yourself), and with a punch needle, you push loops down (away from you). Additionally, as you'll see throughout the book, the projects in this book are made on monks cloth. Traditional rug hooks can be more difficult to use with monks cloth, as the springiness of the weave is less compatible with the tool. That said, it is possible, so don't count it out entirely if it's all you have access to.

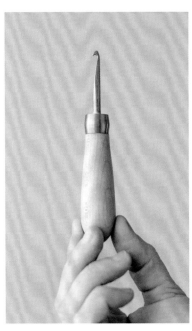

If you'd like to work with a traditional hook, I recommend using linen, or good-quality burlap (for a project other than a floor rug), both available in rug hooking supply stores. These fabrics have less elasticity and aren't as likely to snag the end of the hook.

Pen-Style Punch Needles

Pen-style punch needles are similar to the Lavor. They have adjustable needle lengths and need to be threaded with a wire needle threader. This style works well and is a great option as an inexpensive entry point, but most are made for finer weights of yarn, and therefore aren't well suited to the projects in this particular book. The handles can also be uncomfortable to hold while crafting large pieces. To create the projects in this book, you'll want to choose a punch needle that will accommodate bulky/chunky yarns.

incompatible tools
FOR THE PROJECTS IN THIS BOOK

For more on related crafts, see What Is Punch Needle Rug Hooking? (page 10).

Vintage Shuttle-Style Punch Needles: These tools are often operated with both hands. You alternate pushing each side down into the backing in a back-and-forth motion. Lots of different versions can be found online and in antique shops called a variety of names, including rug hookers, shuttle needles, and speed tufters. In my experience, these tools are a little harder to control with precision, and they generally require an upright frame setup. They are lovely pieces of history though, and are great to collect and experiment with.

Embroidery Punch Needles / Tools Meant for Russian or Miniature Punch: These are punch needles that use very thin, fine materials like embroidery threads and flosses. Punch needle rug hooking typically uses yarns suitable for functional use.

Latch Hooks: These look similar to a traditional rug hook, but with a small latch set underneath the hook. The tool gathers and ties precut pieces of material (yarn or fabric) into a knot on an open weave backing. Rugs made from this tool have a cut pile rather than a looped pile.

Danella Needles: These are a unique eggbeater style of punching tool that are manufactured in Denmark. You can use them with thin yarns to make a functional low-pile rug with great mechanized efficiency. Although this tool works well, the yarn measurements would be different than those listed in this book, as we are using thicker rug yarns.

Locker Hooks: These tools have a hook at one end and a needle eye at the other. They're used to make locker-hooked rugs on a specialized backing with a large open weave. The loops are locked in place using twine.

Vintage Shuttle-Style Punch Needle

Tufting Guns: These tools are by far the fastest rug-making option available, and can be pneumatic or electric. Depending on the gun's features, it can produce a loop or cut pile in a variety of pile heights. Gun-tufted rugs must be glued, and cannot rely on backing tension alone. They can also only accomodate a limited range of yarn weights, usually working best with medium weight yarns.

Basic Tools

Beyond the punch needle itself, the tools you need for this craft are similar to the tools for most textile crafts. Some are specific to the individual projects featured in the book, but most are useful over a wide range of punch needle projects:

• Scissors: I recommend a pair of narrow-tipped scissors for pushing in yarn, and a pair of duckbill scissors for cutting yarn tails flush to the pile, but any pair of scissors will do.

• Pencil

• Black permanent marker (Sharpie)

• Paper for printing/drawing patterns

• Iron

• Ruler

• Cloth or a towel for blocking

• Masking tape

• Hand-sewing needle

• Thimble

• All-purpose thread

• Heavy-duty thread (upholstery thread or button and craft thread)

• Sewing pins

• Tapestry/yarn needle

ADDITIONAL TOOLS

• Sewing machine with a zipper foot (optional)

• Serger or pinking shears (optional)

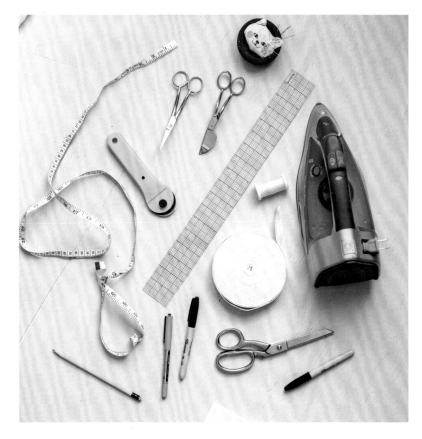

• Carpet adhesive: I recommend Roberts carpet adhesive in numbers 3095 or 6700, found in most hardware stores or online.

• Disposable putty knife or utensil for spreading glue

• Staple gun and staples

• 1″ twill tape or rug binding (Floral Trio Handbag, page 114)

• Packing tape (Home Sweet Home Doorstop, page 84)

• Box cutter (Home Sweet Home Doorstop, page 84)

• Sturdy cardboard (Home Sweet Home Doorstop, page 84)

• Brick or suitably shaped rock/weight (Home Sweet Home Doorstop, page 84)

• Pillow insert or stuffing

• T-pins and blocking mats for blocking

• Rotary cutter

• Fabric shaver or lint roller

MATERIALS

The "right" materials for a punch needle rug hooking project depend on a variety of things. Most importantly, what do you have access to? Don't let price barriers or hard-to-find yarns hold you back from trying this craft. There are solutions (and substitutions) to be found based on your needs. That said, it's important to consider your materials carefully—they are the very substance of your piece, affecting the longevity, look, and feel of what you produce. See Resources (page 142) for information on my favorite brands and places to source materials.

Yarns

Yarns are the main material that make up every punch needle design in this book. The yarn you choose will contribute to the look, quality, and durability of your pieces.

WOOL RUG YARN

Rug yarns are made from 100% wool that is toothy and has a high micron count. A micron is the measurement used to indicate the thickness of the individual wool fibers, which in turn describes its softness. Fine and wearable yarns like merino have a low micron count (around 20), while yarns that are coarser, like rug yarn, have a high micron count (around 30 and higher). This measurement isn't always listed, but it's still a good piece of information to look for when sourcing your materials.

If a yarn is described as being a lovely and soft material, perfect for wearing against the skin, it's unlikely to be suitable for a durable floor rug. Rug yarns are rugged, slightly scratchy, and the absolute best (and easiest) yarns to work with when making functional floor rugs. The scratchy texture allows them to grip nicely onto the rug's backing without slipping out of place, and when loops are formed, they'll cling to one another, securing the overall construction of your finished project. They're also a great deal easier to move on a gripper strip frame in comparison to other options. It's very unlikely you'll mar or snag the beautiful punched loops on gripper needles when they're made from rug yarn—and that's key!

Rug yarns also have a very sturdy structure, making for a resilient pile that will keep its shape for generations. They won't lose plushness over time from the weight of being walked on, nor will they compress too much through the blocking process. These yarns are easy to wash and dye, as they're *much* less prone to felting. Felting happens when wool fibers become tangled together through friction, resulting in a shrunken, matted, and stiff material or yarn. And with all these rugged attributes, 100% wool rug yarn also makes a lovely, squishy, and comfortable surface to sit and stand on.

Another one of my favorite characteristics of wool is that its environmental impacts are quite low. It's a completely natural resource that is renewable, durable, and biodegradable in the long run—properties that cannot be reproduced synthetically. Magic, really!

When searching for materials, you'll find that wool rug yarns generally have a lower sheen than other yarns, meaning they are less light reflective. I personally love this natural, chalky look, and prefer it over other options. All the rugs in this book are punched from 100% wool rug yarn.

HAND-DYED RUG YARNS

Hand-dyeing rug yarns creates a range of colors without comparison. Hand-dyed yarns have lovely, luminescent, semi-solid hues that just can't be replicated by large-batch commercial dyeing. You can dye these yarns yourself, or purchase them from independent makers. They're often sold in variegated colors, with nuanced, tonal shades—but they can come with a high price tag! If artisan dyed yarns aren't within your budget, dyeing them yourself is the way to go, and it's easier than you might think!

Find suppliers of off-white unbleached rug yarn and acid dyes, and give it a go. Acid dyes are textile dyes that come in every color imaginable. They're friendly to use, even for beginner textile artists, and on average, they have good longevity and lightfastness. Acid dyes are well suited to protein fibers like wool and silk, but they even work on nylon. They're water-soluble and easy to set using pantry staples like vinegar or citric acid. Depending on your location, consider reputable brands such as Majic Carpet Dyes, PRO Chemical & Dye, Dharma Trading Co., or Jacquard Products.

For full instructions on using these materials and dyeing your own yarn, see Dyeing Wool Yarns (page 56).

ACRYLIC AND SYNTHETIC YARNS

Acrylic (and other synthetic) yarns are very easy to find, are inexpensive, and come in an amazing range of colors. They are made from a type of plastic, making them water-resistant and resilient against staining. But they can be slippery and difficult to work with, as they're more susceptible to slipping out of the backing and the needle. They may also catch and pull on the gripper strip frame, so if you're using them, be very careful when moving the piece around on the frame.

Be wary of ironing these yarns too, as their fibers will melt at high temperatures. Keep the heat setting low, as directed by your specific iron for synthetic fibers. Since these yarns are made of plastic, I encourage any attempt at sourcing options made from recycled materials or sold through secondhand shops when possible.

PLANT AND ANIMAL FIBER YARNS

Though we already covered wool rug yarns, there are many other types of wool yarns available, along with cotton, bamboo, linen, hemp, and other plant and animal fibers that each have great qualities, sheens, and textures. They offer a lot of character in their look and feel, and are good options for experimenting with when you want to add interest or variation to a punched piece.

Know, though, that the softness of these plant and animal fibers can make for a less hearty loop structure when compared to rug yarn. This is important when considering how the work will be used; while it would be perfect for wall decor, if someone will be walking on the finished piece, these yarns are not always the best choice. Some can be slippery in the backing or snag on the frame too. Soft animal fibers will also felt if not washed carefully, making them less practical for daily use.

YARN WEIGHT

For our purposes, to achieve a thick loopy pile, I recommend using a bulky-weight yarn—otherwise known as *chunky yarn* or *craft yarn*, and sometimes it can be labeled as *rug yarn*. Bulky yarns come in a wide range of plies, so don't let the ply number confuse you. A yarn's ply refers to the number of strands twisted together. But the individual strands can vary in diameter, so ply isn't a great way to measure the total thickness of a yarn. Instead, look for keywords like *bulky* and *chunky* in the description.

Some yarns have a numerical measurement on the label that refers to the yarn's weight. A lace weight yarn is 0 and a bulky weight yarn is 5. You can also gauge the correct weight by looking at the recommended size of knitting needles. For chunky/bulky yarn, needle sizes US 10–US 11 (6.0mm–8.0mm) are usually recommended.

Some yarns are also described by their WPI, or wraps per inch. Bulky yarns measure roughly 6–7 WPI. To calculate this measurement, hold a length of yarn in one hand and a pencil in the other. Wrap the yarn around the pencil in one layer using consistent tension. Continue for a few inches, then count how many wraps fit into 1″ (2.5cm).

If you're buying yarn online and are having difficulty discerning the weight, consult websites like Ravelry. Ravelry has an enormous catalog of information on yarn brands, with weights and other traits listed. I use Briggs & Little Super 4 Ply yarn for all the projects in this book. It's a bulky yarn, available in many colors or unbleached white, which is perfect for hand-dyeing. It's an affordable option available throughout Canada and the United States. For a full list of recommended rug yarns, see Resources (page 142).

Can thinner yarns be used to punch functional rugs? Absolutely! But the number of stitches per inch while punching and yarn usage calculations will be different from those used in this book, and the visual look of the finished piece will be different as well. Make sure to use a punch needle that accommodates the weight of yarn you're using.

Backing Materials

A backing material is the fabric you punch the yarn into, providing the foundation and strength that holds the work together. It keeps the loops secure through tension in its woven structure. Backings are sold by many retailers, but I would recommend finding a reputable dealer (make sure to look local!) who sells your preferred high-quality fabric. If you're unsure about quality, read reviews online or tap into punch needle and rug hooking groups on social media. The crafting community is full of experienced makers who are happy to help with suggestions in your area.

MONKS CLOTH

The backing I recommend for all the projects in this book is monks cloth, especially if you're using a rug hooking or gripper strip frame (more on frames later in this chapter). Monks cloth is very strong, easy to work with, and (relatively) inexpensive. It has an open weave, so there will be small holes between the warp and weft for you to punch through. Make sure to use the monks cloth sized especially for punch needle, with twelve to fourteen holes per inch. Some brands of monks cloth are woven too loosely, so it's likely that loops won't stay in place, or the overall integrity of your work will be compromised.

Monks cloth is 100% cotton, so it won't melt due to ironing, and it is very forgiving if you make a mistake: Simply pull out the yarn, then use your punch needle to quickly push and pull the warp and weft bands back to their original positions. Some brands of monks cloth feature horizontal grid lines, a very helpful feature when you want to ensure your design is square. I use Dorr Mill brand monks cloth, which is readily available through quality rug hooking and punch needle supply shops.

A possible downside to monks cloth is the stretchiness caused by the open weave and material. While I don't personally find it to be a hassle, you may need to retighten the backing through the punching process. Retightening is easy if you're using a gripper or nonslip hoop frame, but it's a big chore if you're using a canvas stretcher bar frame with the backing stapled.

RUG WARP

Although popular among many punch needle artists, rug warp is admittedly not my favorite option for backing. I like that it's sturdy and 100% cotton, but it's woven more tightly than monks cloth and requires a lot of exertion to punch bulky yarns through it. It's an excellent choice for finer, worsted-weight yarns, and is a great quality backing. When rug warp is used to make a floor rug, it will provide a strong foundation and have no trouble keeping the loops secure.

RUG HOOKING LINEN

Rug hooking linen is a favorite among traditional rug hookers, but it also works very well with punch needle. Made from flax, this backing is exceptionally strong, and the weave holds loops securely in place.

Because it's more rigid than monks cloth, it makes a good backing option when you're using a canvas stretcher bar frame—you won't have to worry as much about losing tension while working. But the higher cost of this backing might negate any money you save by using a stretcher bar frame—it's the most expensive of all the backing options.

Be sure to choose a linen appropriate for rug hooking in a weave that matches your weight of yarn. Consider the number of threads per square inch. When working with a bulky weight yarn, choose a linen that has about 12 × 12 threads per square inch. This is sometimes called *primitive linen*, but always make sure to check the actual thread count. A weave with more than this number of threads is better suited to thinner yarns. Rug hooking linen can readily be found in rug hooking and punch needle rug hooking supply shops.

BURLAP

Burlap has the endorsement of many punch needle artists, but I don't recommend it myself if you're making functional items. It's made from jute fibers that are prone to breaking down when exposed to moisture, and it just doesn't hold up well in the long run. Burlap is a fine backing for making decorative pieces with a traditional rug hook, but it's not well suited to punch needle rug hooking, especially when making floor rugs.

FRAMES

Frames *can* be an expensive part of getting into punch needle, with prices ranging anywhere from $15 to $700. But there are lots of options, so you're sure to find something to suit your needs, level of interest, and budget.

Gripper Strip Frames

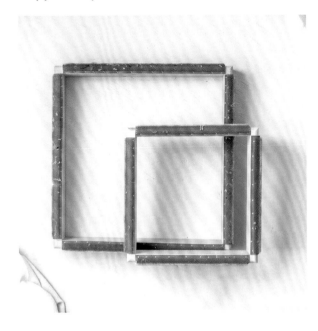

Gripper strip frames feature strips of fine, outward-leaning needles tacked on all sides of a solid wooden frame. These needles, called *grippers*, do a really great job of holding the backing in place until you need to move it on or off the frame. The frames come in a variety of sizes, and are easily one of the best investments you can make. I also recommend getting an elasticized frame cover, which will protect your arms and hands from the sharp needles while you punch.

Look for a gripper strip frame deep enough that when you punch, the needle will not hit the table or work surface below. If the frame isn't deep enough, you'll need to lean the frame or prop it against something taller, giving you more working space on the pile side.

If your budget is tight or you want a custom size, you can also make your own; you can easily find gripper strips online and attach them to a wooden frame with nails or staples.

I recommend purchasing (or making) a medium-size gripper strip frame, around 18″ × 18″ or 20″ × 20″. The frame does not have to be square, and any dimensions around this size will suit you well as a beginner. It's not too big for medium-size projects, and yet it's still big enough to punch a good-size area before having to shift the piece on the frame.

If you're using sturdy rug yarn, you do *not* need to purchase a gripper strip frame the size of the finished project. Instead, you can remove the project from the frame and shift its placement to work on a new area. Large and table-size frames are lovely to have, but aren't necessary. You'll also see special stands to hold your frame at different heights and angles, but truthfully, my favorite way to work is curled up in a comfy chair with a gripper strip frame that's deep enough to set directly on my lap.

Stretcher Bar Frames

Making a frame from canvas stretcher bars is a low-commitment option if you're testing your interest in the craft. It's best to choose a frame that is equal to or bigger than the dimensions of your intended project, since moving the backing around on the frame is quite difficult with this frame type, and is likely to damage the rug. Remember, too, that monks cloth can stretch while punching, so crafting a large rug on this sort of frame can lead to frustration after the initial fabric tension is lost. A smaller piece will be less affected.

Working with a stretcher bar frame is a great way to display the finished work too—keep it on the frame and hang it directly onto the wall without any sewing or hemming required (see Framed Flowers Wall Hanging, page 98)! Removing a finished piece from the frame is always an option too; just make sure you take your time when removing the staples to avoid any damage to the backing.

Purchase stretcher bars at your preferred dimensions, assemble them with the notches, and hammer them together with a mallet or hammer.

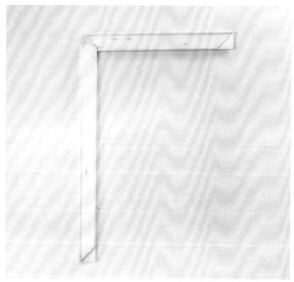

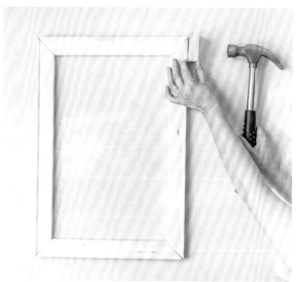

Cut a piece of backing that extends 2″ larger than the frame on all sides. Lay the backing fabric underneath the frame. Fold it over the wood to the top side, as shown. Staple the backing down along one side of the frame. Then, on the opposite side of the frame, pull tightly on the backing as you fold it over. The fabric should be as taut as a drum. Start in the middle, stapling the taut backing to the frame, and then continue to both corners. Repeat on the other two sides.

If you're using the frame for display, splay the excess corner fabric down against the frame as neatly as possible, and staple it down flat so that the finished piece will hang flush against the wall.

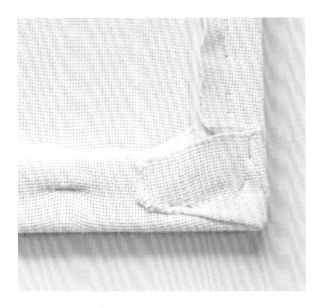

Nonslip Punch Needle Hoops

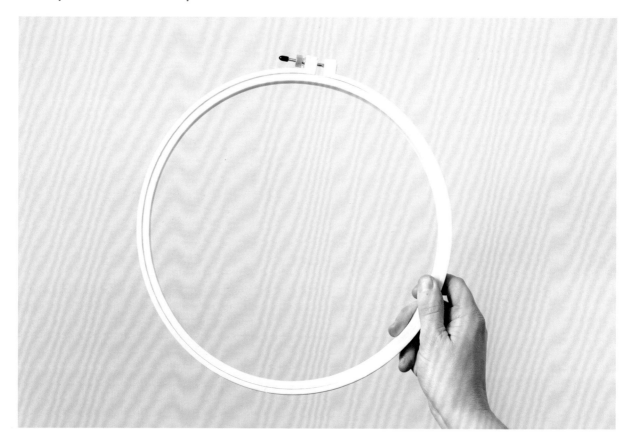

Punch needle hoops are economical, easy to store, and a good option for your smallest projects, like coasters or small wall hangings. Make sure you find a quality hoop that specifically works well with a punch needle—standard embroidery hoops aren't up to the task of keeping the backing fabric taut for trouble-free punching. Instead you'll want to find a brand capable of holding good tension in the fabric. A couple of options include the Morgan No-Slip Hoop or the Susan Bates embroidery hoop with a Super Grip lip.

Carpet Tack Frames

Carpet tack frames are similar to gripper strip frames, but instead they have rows of sharp tacks spaced farther apart than gripper needles. They are a cost-effective option and can be easily assembled using materials from hardware stores or online retailers, but are arguably less convenient and user-friendly overall when compared to gripper strip frames, as the tacks aren't as well distributed as grippers. To make one, nail carpet tack strips facing outward to all four sides of a wooden frame. When using a carpet tack frame, it's very important to protect your arms from scratches, so after stretching the backing taut over the tacks, pad the frame with a rolled piece of fabric or foam and work cautiously to avoid injury.

Chéticamp Frames

A Chéticamp frame is a beautiful table-style frame. When working on it, you'll sit in a chair as you would at a desk. The advantage with this frame is in being able to see more of the work at once due to a larger punching area. You also don't have to work around sharp grippers. Instead, the backing is sewn onto strips of canvas that are attached to long wooden rods. You then roll the strips taut, therefore tightening one axis of the backing with the rods. The two remaining sides are tightened through different means, depending on the style of Chéticamp frame.

When working on a large rug, you can simply roll the finished/punched area onto a rod, unroll the unfinished portion from the other rod, and continue working. This eliminates the need to shift the work around on the frame as you punch. These frames can be expensive and relatively hard to find. But if you're in the market for one, look at secondhand markets online or in historic rug hooking communities through Canada and the Eastern United States. For more on Chéticamp, see Looking Back (page 11).

SETTING UP

PREPARING THE BACKING

With an iron, press the cloth backing smooth and flat. I recommend finishing the edges of the backing to prevent fraying and tangling. You can do this by zigzag stitching around the perimeter with a sewing machine, serging the edges with a serger, or taping them using masking or painter's tape. If you choose the third method, simply tape around the perimeter of the backing, then flip it over and repeat, sandwiching the edges of the cloth between two layers of tape.

If you're wondering how much yarn to prepare for an original design, see Calculating Yarn and Backing Amounts (page 67). Each project in this book includes required yarn yardage.

Transferring the Pattern

My favorite transfer method is simple. Print or draw the pattern onto paper. If necessary, tape paper pattern pieces together. Then, using masking tape, affix the paper pattern to a bright large window. This must be done during the day, so light shines through the pattern. This can also be done with a lightbox.

Tape the backing (ideally monks cloth) over the pattern (masking and painter's tape work best). The backing should be 5″ larger than the design on all sides so that there is room to secure it onto a frame. To ensure the design is straight, line up one of the cloth's grid lines with a horizontal or vertical pattern line. Or if you prefer, mark a level horizontal line 5″ from the top of the backing fabric with a pencil, then use this line as a guide for lining up the backing on the paper pattern. It's important to ensure the pattern lines you draw are level and straight.

Now it's time to trace the pattern! Start with any straight lines in the pattern, and use the fabric weave as a guide. Then fill in the rest of the lines, tracing the entire pattern. You won't see these markings through the rug pile, so little "mistakes" really aren't a big deal. Note that any design transferred this way will result in a final punched piece that is a mirror image of the original design.

The patterns in this book are provided as a digital download file. To access them for printing, scan the QR code or access the tinyurl in Projects (page 68).

SETTING UP A GRIPPER STRIP FRAME

Lay the backing fabric over the frame, with the area where you will begin punching set in the middle. A little at a time, pull two sides of the fabric over the grippers, tightening the backing evenly. Pull the other two sides, and continue tightening all sides until the fabric is taut like a drum. Gradually stretching the fabric ensures that the pattern doesn't stretch too far in one direction and become distorted. If you have a frame cover, slide it over the gripper spikes to protect your arms. The frame is ready!

THREADING A PUNCH NEEDLE

Threading Oxford and Craftsman's Style Punch Needles

1 Find the tail of the yarn, and thread it through the eye of the needle. *fig. A*

2 Hold the yarn tail with one hand, and run the yarn through the channel in the handle with the other. Pull it down into the channel, tugging it into place. *fig. B*

3 Pull the yarn back and forth, ensuring it is nestled in the channel and glides smoothly without catching. *fig. C*

Threading Lavor, Tube-Style, and Pen-Style Needles

1 Find the tail of the yarn. Grab a long wire needle threader, and insert it through the needle (into the tip and out of the base of the needle). The closed loop of the needle threader should be at the base of the needle. *fig. D*

2 Insert the yarn into the loop of the wire, folding it over and pulling the tail through a bit. *fig. E*

3 Pull the top of the wire threader, bringing the yarn up through the needle. Remove the wire threader. Unfold the yarn so the tail is loose at the top of the needle. *fig. F*

4 Thread the tail of the yarn through the eye of the needle. If necessary, adjust the needle to the appropriate length for ¼" loops. Pull the yarn back and forth, ensuring it glides smoothly through the needle without catching. *fig. G*

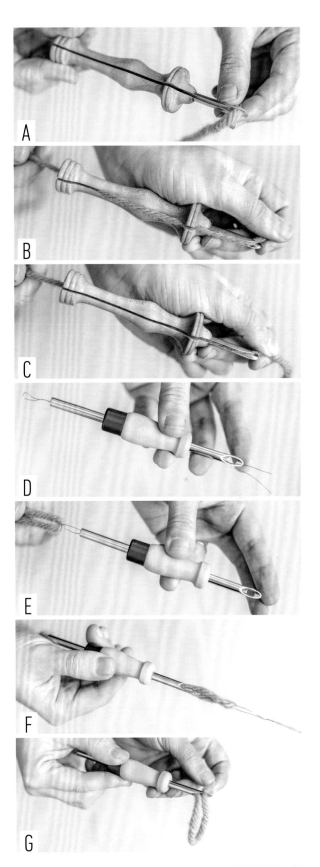

A

B

C

D

E

F

G

PUNCH NEEDLE RUG HOOKING BASICS

The techniques in this chapter are all you need to create a beautiful and sturdy punched rug. I've detailed the process step by step, but know that once you've gotten the hang of the basics, you'll master the craft quickly and easily. Part of the fun of punch needle rug hooking is that it's so simple! With a bit of practice, you'll be punching like a professional.

PUNCHING A ROW OF STITCHES

1 Hold the punch needle as you would a pencil. The channel on the handle (if there is one) should be pointed in the direction you're stitching. Insert the needle into the fabric backing. Push the needle all the way down until the handle reaches the backing. Make sure that with every stitch, you are consistently pushing the needle all the way down to create even loops through the project. *fig. A*

2 Pull the needle out, but keep the tip of the needle touching the fabric. Do not pull it out farther. Drag it along the backing and into the position of the next stitch. Push the needle back down into the fabric. *fig. B*

note

Pulling the needle away from the backing will pull up on the prior stitches. This might make the loop sizes uneven, or it might even pull out the stitch completely. Keep the needle as close to the backing as possible while punching.

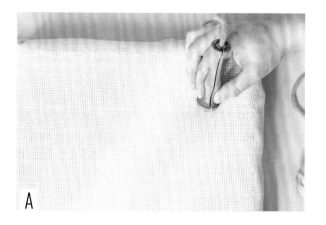

A

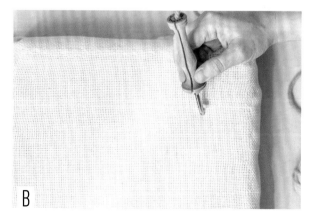

B

3 Repeat Steps 1 and 2, punching the needle all the way into the backing, pulling it up so the needle tip rests on the fabric, dragging it forward to the next stitch location, and punching again. Steer the needle by pointing the channel on the handle (if there is one) in the direction of each upcoming stitch.

4 To finish an area of stitches, whether you need to change yarns or start punching in a new location, lift the needle like normal, then pinch the yarn at the base of the just completed stitch, preventing it from pulling out of the backing. Lift the needle away, and cut the yarn about ¼″ above the backing. *fig. C*

5 Using the punch needle or the closed tip of a small pair of scissors, poke the yarn tail from Step 4 into its hole to the loop side of the project. You may need to poke it 3–5 times, pressing and smooshing the tail down, until it pops through to the other side. Pushing tails in helps lock the stitches into place, so don't skip this step when making functional items. *fig. D*

6 Flip the work over so the loop side is facing up. Hold the tail loosely, then trim it flush with the height of the pile. Don't put tension on the tail as you hold it up, or you may accidentally cut it too short. *fig. E*

TIP Pushing tails to the loop side will result in a more secure rug. Not doing so may lead to a rug with stitches that are more easily pulled out while cleaning or with wear. You may choose to push tails in as you go or, if you're like me, you can save this task until the end of the project and push all the tails in at once. If you save this step for the end of the project, you may need to go back and punch new stitches to fill in any gap left by the tails. When filling small gaps, punch a minimum of three stitches for a secure set of loops.

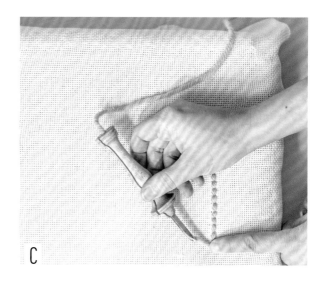

C

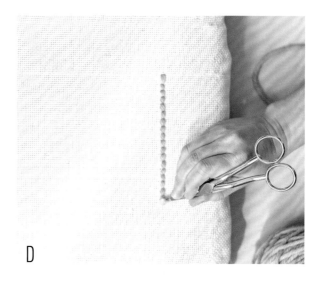

D

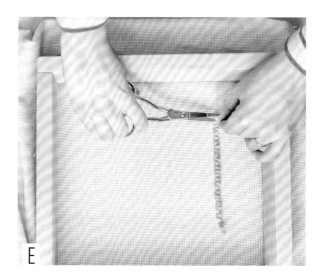

E

OUTLINING AND TRACING

Many patterns may require you to trace a shape or create an outline while punching. Punch approximately six stitches per inch (when using bulky yarn) to create a crisp, defined border line for these areas. I call this *border stitching*.

With some designs, it's also helpful to outline *the exterior* of the same shape with a second row of border stitches. This will help reinforce the definition of the initial border stitch line. This second row should match the color of the exterior shape. For example, in the Playmates Floor Mat (page 108), I outline and fill the border oval shapes in dark brown. Then when I begin filling in the background color, I start by adding a second layer of reinforcing border stitches around the same ovals using the background color.

Unlike fill stitches (see page 38), border stitches do not need to be *staggered* against adjoining border stitches. Instead, aligning the two rows of border stitches with one another will help reinforce a crisp line. Perfection isn't necessary here; just keep this principle in mind while working if you are aiming for crisp definition.

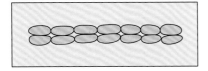

Avoid adding a second layer of border stitches if your design is at risk of being *overpacked* (see page 39).

Border stitching the Floral Trivet (page 70)

FILLING SHAPES AND BACKGROUNDS

When you fill in shapes and background areas, use a wider stitch length—roughly four stitches per inch. *Fill stitches* leave some breathing room in the backing, allowing the rug pile to lay flat. If you used border stitches for an entire rug, it would both overuse yarn and overpack the backing.

How you fill a shape is ultimately up to you. Some artists punch in a spiral until an area has been filled, while others work back and forth. If possible, avoid creating one area with a cluster of tails, and make sure to avoid jumping over previous stitches. Jumping over stitches adds bulk under the rug, and creates stress points that will wear the yarn out faster.

STAGGERING STITCHES

To achieve a full-looking pile without gaps or exposed fabric on the loop side of a rug, punch fill stitches like a row of bricks, with the ends of one stitch in the center of the stitch above or below it.

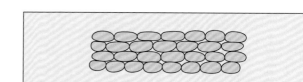

This method should be applied most importantly to fill stitches. Don't worry if the layout isn't always perfect; just keep this principle in mind, using it as a general rule while you punch.

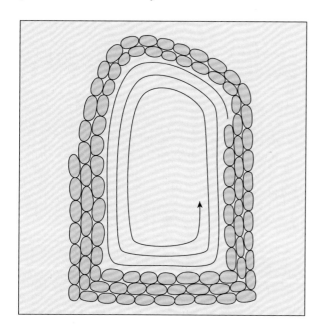

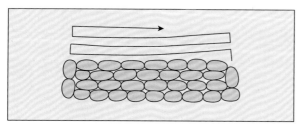

BALANCING STITCH DENSITY

When stitches are punched too densely over an area, the area tends to buckle, and it creates lumps along the rug's surface, preventing it from lying flat on the floor or the wall. In contrast, when stitches are punched too loosely, the rug pile will look sparse and the backing will show. This also compromises the rug's structural integrity, since its strength relies on the tension between loops. The right balance is somewhere in the middle.

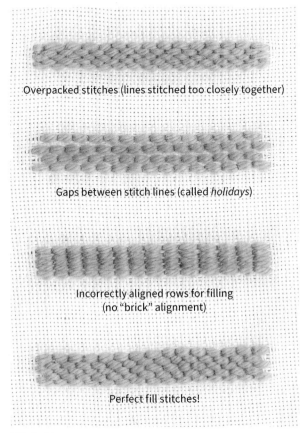

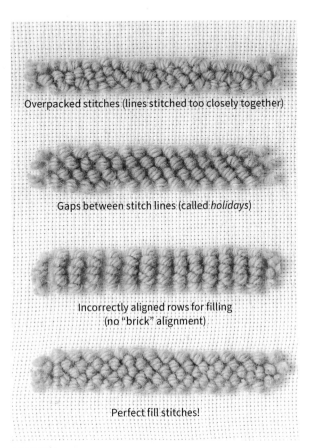

Overpacked stitches (lines stitched too closely together)

Gaps between stitch lines (called *holidays*)

Incorrectly aligned rows for filling (no "brick" alignment)

Perfect fill stitches!

Stitch side

Loop side

troubleshooting

HEAR AN UNUSUAL "CRUNCH" SOUND AFTER PUNCHING?

Either you've broken a thread in the backing, or a stitch has become entangled within another loop. No big deal! If you notice a tangled loop, you can tease it out on the loop side when you're tidying loops at the end of a project. The odd broken thread in the backing will not affect the punching.

DO THE LOOPS LOOK UNEVEN OR LOOSE?

There are a few reasons this might happen. If you don't have enough slack in the ball of yarn you're using, the high tension may be preventing the yarn from moving freely, which means the needle cannot make proper-size loops. Similarly, a knot or other obstruction might be keeping the yarn from feeding smoothly through the needle. Make sure it's gliding smoothly.

If you're working with slippery yarn, this might be an issue too. Consider switching to a coarse yarn, like the recommended wool rug yarn. Finally, if you're using a very loosely woven backing, you may encounter the same issues, and you should choose a backing better suited for punch needle rug hooking.

DOES THE FINISHED PIECE CURL OR BUBBLE?

If your piece doesn't lie flat after blocking, you'll want to pull out the areas that are most affected and repunch them. Pay close attention to your stitch density. If it's a highly detailed design (unlike the patterns in this book), try using just one row of border stitches instead of two.

FIXING MISTAKES

One of my favorite things about punch needle rug hooking is how easily "mistakes" can be corrected. You can experiment as much as you want without wasting materials. This is especially true when using monks cloth as the backing—it's such a forgiving fabric, as the warp and weft threads can easily be pushed back into place without damage.

To remove an area of yarn, simply pull on a tail from the *stitch* side of the piece, or pull on a stitch itself. As soon as you get it loose, you can easily pull the stitches out.

After removing the yarn, use the tip of the punch needle or the closed tip of your scissors to move the warp and weft of the backing back into their original position. You'll still be able to tell the area has been previously punched, but the backing isn't compromised—it's ready to be worked up again in whatever way you choose!

If the yarn you've pulled out is kinked or zigzagged, simply soak it in hot water to reset its shape. Hang it to dry.

MOVING ON A GRIPPER STRIP FRAME

As you work on larger projects, you'll likely need to move the piece around on the gripper strip frame. Like I mentioned, you don't need a frame that's larger than your project; you just need to adjust the piece's positioning on the frame. It is easiest to move a rug punched with rug yarn or coarse wool yarn. Softer, more slippery, or more delicate yarns are much more likely to stick to the gripper strip frame. If you are using delicate yarns, try adding a layer of Glad Press'n Seal to the areas of the rug that will be set over the grippers to reduce some of the pulling against the loops.

To move a project punched with rug wool on a gripper strip frame, start by loosening the tension: Release the backing from one side of the frame by pulling it *away* from the needles, *up* off the frame, then release it completely. From here it should be easy to peel or roll the project toward the opposite end of the frame until it is completely off.

Reposition the piece so the desired (unpunched) area is on the frame. If a punched section needs to go over the needles, stabilize the loops by holding your hand over them on the stitch side, pressing down as you pull the fabric toward the opposite row of grippers. Then repeat on all remaining sides, stabilizing the loops whenever they overlap the gripper strips and tightening the backing until the tension is even on all sides. If the loops are overlapping more than one side of the gripper strip frame, simply take turns, stabilizing the loops on one side and tightening the opposite side. The Bird in the Garden Floor Rug (page 74) also walks you through the process of moving the piece on the frame.

BLOCKING AND TIDYING LOOPS

Before moving on to these finishing steps, make sure to push all yarn tails to the loop side and trim them flush with the pile (see Punching a Row of Stitches, page 34).

Tidying Loops

During punching, rows tend to settle into one another, creating blended shapes instead of clean lines between colors. After you finish stitching a whole project, tidying the loops will magically transform your fuzzy design into a clear and crisp one. With a narrow pair of scissors or the punch needle, simply move the loops (on the loop side of the piece) into their desired positions.

To form clean lines along pattern shapes, I find it helpful to push one row of loops in one direction (using the pointy end of a narrow pair of scissors) while pushing the abutting row of loops in the other direction (with my finger). Continue tidying loops through the blocking process, as heat makes the yarn loops much more malleable.

You may also need to cut some loops. If you unintentionally have a few odd loops that are taller than others, don't fret! Simply cut them flush with the rest of the pile. As long as this area is surrounded by other whole loops, the tension will easily still support the cut loops. After blocking, I like to run my hand over the surface of a finished rug, looking for small lumps and bumps; these are often areas where a tail didn't make it through to the pile side and is instead compacted within the pile. Rub the pile with your finger or the punch needle to tease the tail out, then trim it.

Blocking

Blocking is an important step in achieving a uniform and professional look. It is the process of setting the yarn into your desired position and shape. It can be helpful to block projects twice, both before and after finishing, though I often block larger rugs several times. It's important to note that synthetic and delicate yarns are prone to having their loops squished or flattened while blocking. Even worse, some are likely to melt under the heat of an iron, so block carefully and with low heat if you're using these yarns. Block wool rug yarns with higher heat, as per the directions on your iron.

First, lay the rug flat, loop side up, over a heatproof surface. Lay a damp towel over the loop side of the project. Heat an iron to the setting appropriate for the yarn, and then set it onto the damp towel, allowing it to steam each area thoroughly. Move the iron over the whole rug, repeating this process. The heat and steam will relax the stitches, allowing the rug to lay nice and flat. I like to lift the towel and tidy loops as I steam, while the loops are still warm and malleable.

After you've finished any hemming or sewing required for the project, it's often helpful to do a final blocking. Continue tidying loops as you press the piece into the desired shape. Repeat the same process, blocking until all the loops have been set. A hooked rug should lay flat, without any curling, rising, or buckling (unless you've intentionally punched those textures!). Once pressed, allow the piece to dry in place. This can take more than 24 hours.

You can also use blocking to correct the shape of the piece. Block the piece, then allow it to dry over a pinnable surface, like foam, a heavy rug, or blocking mats. Press the piece into the desired shape, and pin along the entire perimeter, holding it in that shape while it dries.

FINISHING

Finishing techniques allow you to securely finish your work so it can go on to adorn your home. The kind of finishing technique you choose is up to you, and may also vary based on how you'll be using the finished piece. Whipstitching and hemming are a great way to finish pieces that will be used as floor rugs or as wall hangings.

Glue

Whether or not you should finish the back of a piece with glue can be a contentious subject. The popularity of tufting guns has overlapped with the punch needle and rug hooking communities, causing some confusion over this method. Gun-tufted rugs must be glued, but hand-hooked rugs (both traditional rug hooking and punch needle rug hooking) are held securely together through tension. They really do not need to be glued.

There are some instances where glue can be very helpful—there are even two of those examples in this book! But in general, I wouldn't recommend gluing the back of a floor rug. Glue can lead to damage down the road, as many glues eat away at wool fibers. It'll make it more difficult to wash and for dirt to pass through when you shake it out. And if a piece of yarn does come loose or an area of the rug needs to be fixed due to damage (like a stain), glue-backed rugs are extremely difficult to repair, whereas an unglued rug can be very easily repunched.

Hemming

Hemming the back of a floor rug or a decorative rug by folding and sewing the backing is a sturdy and professional way to finish a project. The method described here is how I finish all of my floor rugs, and it has proven to hold up very well against daily use.

If a project is meant for the floor, or receives regular use, it is a good idea to use a heavy-duty thread like upholstery or button and craft thread; these threads are built for extra durability and are still fine enough to thread through a regular sewing needle. Decorative pieces like wall hangings can be sewn with standard all-purpose thread.

On rugs that are doormat size or larger, I suggest a finished hem that measures roughly 2″ once sewn. For these rugs, cut a 3″ border of backing fabric around the entire perimeter of the rug. Fold the raw edge under 1″, then again by 2″ to encase the raw edge.

On smaller rugs, a smaller hem is more suitable, so in those cases I recommend a finished hem that measures roughly 1½″. Cut a 2″ border of backing fabric around the entire perimeter of the rug, then fold the raw edge under ½″ and fold it a second time to encase the edge.

Finished hemming

1 With the project lying flat
   on the floor, pile side up,
cut the backing to size around
the perimeter of the piece, as
indicated on page 44 (3″ for larger
rugs, 2″ for smaller rugs).

2 Turn the piece over so the
   stitch side is facing up. Trim
off all four corners, leaving 1″ of
backing at each corner. Begin
creating a mitered corner by
folding the corners in to overlap
the stitch side of the work, and
press with the iron. *figs. A-B*

3 On all four sides, fold the
   backing toward the piece (1″
on large rugs, ½″ on small rugs).
Press. Repeat, folding all four sides
a second time to encase the raw
edge (2″ on large rugs, 1½″ on
small rugs). Neatly align the two
folded edges of the hems in each
corner, creating a mitered corner.
Make sure the monks cloth is not
visible from the pile side of the
rug, but don't pull it tight enough
to curl the edges of the rug. Pin in
place. *fig. C*

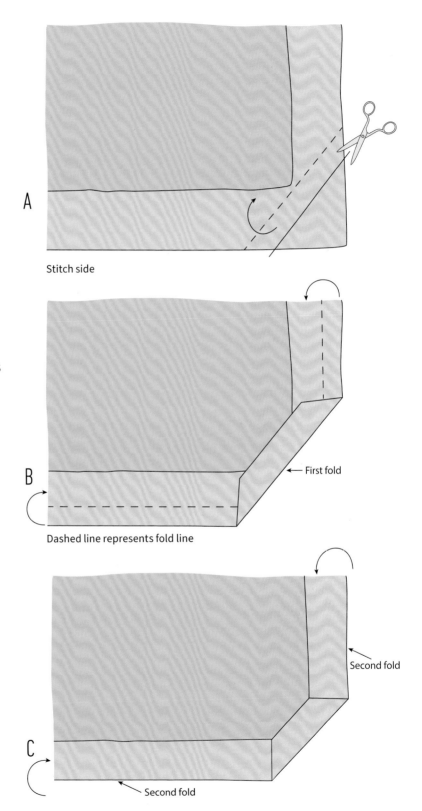

A

Stitch side

B

Dashed line represents fold line

← First fold

C

Second fold

Second fold

4 Whipstitch the straight sides of the backing in place, stitching directly into the rug with a hand-sewing needle and thread (see Whipstitch, page 48). Stitch every 1/2″ or so. Sew mitered corners at all four corners (see Mitered Corners, page 50). *fig. D*

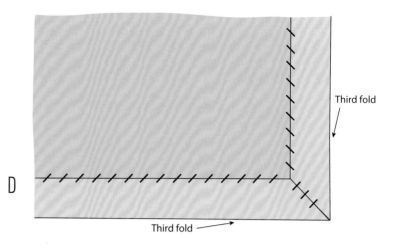

D

Third fold

Third fold

Whipstitching with Yarn

Another way to finish a rug is to whipstitch around the perimeter of the project with yarn. I've used a variation of this technique to close the sides of the Floral Trio Handbag (page 114) and the Changing Weather Clutch (page 136). It's a great way to finish the edges and conceal the backing fabric in a very organic way.

You can also use it in place of hemming to finish a rug, though a standard hem is my finishing preference. To whipstitch around a rug, cut away excess backing, leaving 1½" of fabric around the whole perimeter of the project. Double-fold the raw edge (fold ½", then fold ½" again, enclosing the raw edge), which leaves ½" of folded backing visible from the pile side that will act as the structure under the yarn. As you whipstitch, encase the remaining monks cloth in the yarn.

Thread a yarn needle, and push it into the ½" of backing from the stitch side, directly along (almost within) the exterior line of punched loops. Pull the needle and yarn through, leaving a 2" tail on the stitch side. Bring the needle back to the stitch side, and insert it directly next to the first stitch.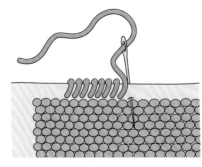
Pull the yarn securely around the edge of the perimeter, but not so tight that you warp the backing. Repeat, creating a solid border of stitches. Tuck the yarn tail into the stitches as you work. Make sure the stitches are close enough together to conceal the backing.

WALL HANGINGS

Many traditional rug hookers sew a channel in the backing for a dowel rod when they intend for the piece to be a wall hanging. With this method, the rug drapes nicely away from the wall, highlighting its tactile quality and dimension. If you choose this method, make sure your rug is well blocked and does not curl.

My preferred method is a little more direct; I love when a rug lies flush against the wall without any evidence of a hanging system. So I simply tap a few nails directly through the rug (in between loops) and into the wall behind it, concealing the nail heads within the pile of the rug. Disperse the weight of the rug among a few nails. I love the minimal look this method achieves, with no visible hardware or hanging devices.

rug backing

Do you need to add backing to your rug? Nope! In fact, adding another layer of fabric to the back of a floor rug will make it harder to clean. If you want to prevent it from sliding on the floor, place a separate nonslip rug pad underneath instead.

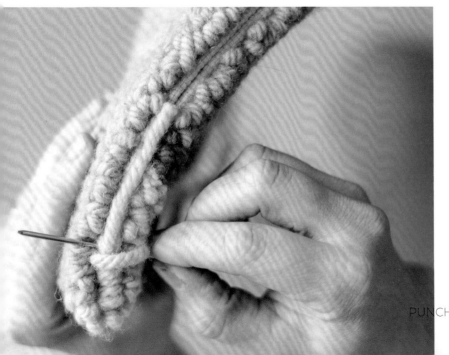

HAND-SEWING STITCH GUIDE

When finishing a punch needle piece, you'll need to do some hand sewing. So I've included a quick guide to hand sewing and the basic stitches we use in this book.

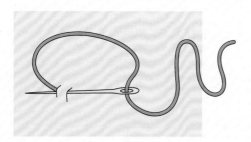

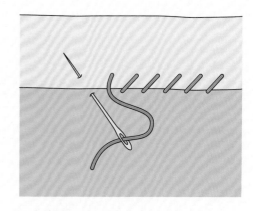

ANCHORING THREAD

I don't like to fuss around with tying knots in my thread. Instead, I start any hand sewing by anchoring the thread. To do this, make a tiny straight stitch (going through only two or three threads of the backing/ fabric). Start by going up through the back of the project, and leave a 1″ tail on the backside. Instead of pulling the tiny stitch taut, leave a loop on the right side of the project. Then, start a second stitch by bringing the needle up through the same point as the first stitch. Thread the needle under the loop of the first stitch, and pull the thread taut. Then, finish the stitch by putting the needle down through the fabric in the same place the first stitch ended. For extra security, I often do this a second time.

WHIPSTITCH

Whipstitch is used in almost all finishing techniques, whether to hem the piece or finish it completely with yarn (see Finishing, page 44). Whipstitches are used at the edge of a piece, whether that's the folded hem or the perimeter of the backing.

To whipstitch hemmed backing to a rug, start by anchoring the thread. On the stitch side, push the needle through the rug and the folded backing, capturing the edge of the hem. Move ½″ along the piece, then repeat to make a second whipstitch. Continue whipstitching around the rug until you reach a corner.

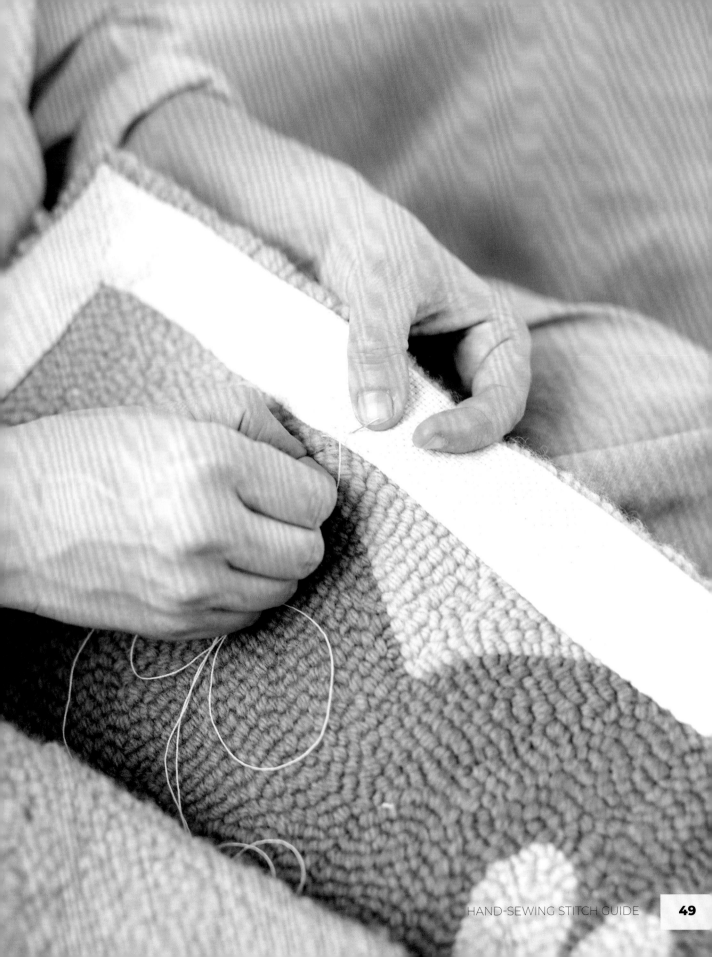

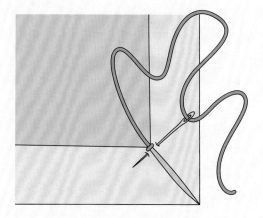

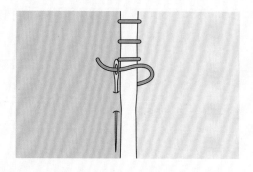

MITERED CORNERS

A mitered corner is a clean way to finish the hemmed corners of a punch needle piece, and avoids unnecessary bulk from overlapping folds. For instructions on folding a mitered corner, see Hemming (page 44). If the corner isn't perfectly aligned, adjust the hems slightly so that both folds are parallel before stitching.

Anchor the thread to the backing. Stitch across the two folded hems at the bottom corner, connecting the two sides. Using a whipstitch or a ladder stitch, sew the two folded edges together from one end to the other. Pull the stitches tight enough that the folded edges meet, but not tightly enough to pucker the seams. Stitch over the final stitch twice for extra security.

LADDER STITCH

The ladder stitch is helpful when joining two sides of fabric, like when closing a small opening on something like a pillow. It's invisible when used to join two folded edges.

To join the two folded pieces of fabric, anchor the thread and insert your needle into the fold of one fabric, bringing the thread out right at the fold.

Then insert the needle into the fold of the other fabric, directly across from where you last pulled the needle out. Slide the needle inside the fold and bring it out ¼" from the last point of insertion, again right at the fold. Repeat this step across the whole gap, pulling each stitch tight to close the seam. If you prefer, you can use a ladder stitch instead of a whipstitch for sewing mitered corners.

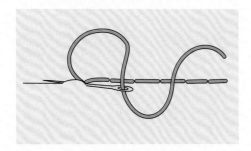

BACKSTITCH

A backstitch is a simple hand-sewing straight stitch for securing two pieces of fabric. If you have or prefer using a sewing machine, you may not need to use a backstitch.

Anchor the thread to the backing. Push the needle through the fabric from back to front. Move forward about ¼″ and push the needle through the fabric from front to back, creating one stitch. Under the fabric, move forward ¼″, and push the needle through the fabric from back to front. Then insert the needle through the previous hole of insertion (the end point of the first stitch) from front to back. This creates two stitches that share one point of insertion. Repeat this process to continue backstitching.

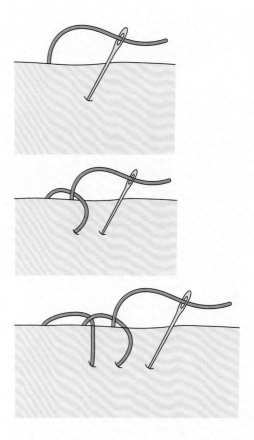

BLANKET STITCH

A blanket stitch is often used to finish a raw edge of a project. It's a great finish on the Butterfly Collar (page 90). Anchor the thread on the back side of the fabric. Lift the needle to the front side of the fabric about ¼″ from the edge and the anchor stitch (or knot), and stitch from front to back to create the first stitch. Thread the needle through the loop of the first stitch, bring it back to the front side, and push it through from front to back ¼″ away to create the second stitch. Repeat, threading the needle through the previous stitch and then creating a new stitch ¼″ away, to blanket stitch the entire edge.

CARING FOR
HAND-HOOKED RUGS

Let me begin by admitting how much I *love* the look of a well-worn hooked rug; the patina that comes with age and use is so special, and it's nearly impossible to replicate except through time and wear. This is not to dissuade you from trying to maintain the original finish of your rug, but a reminder that the little spots and discoloration that can happen over time have a beauty of their own. With this in mind, know that keeping a hand-hooked rug clean is very possible.

These care tips apply best to rugs made with rug yarns on the backings recommended by this book.

GENERAL MAINTENANCE

Vacuum the rug as needed, but avoid using any damaging tools like the rotating brush many vacuums feature. Periodically give the rug a shake outdoors to remove dust and dirt. If the rug develops a fuzzy finish over time from vacuuming or age, give it a once-over with a lint remover or lint shaver to freshen the overall look.

 TIP Keep the rug away from prolonged direct sunlight to prevent the colors from fading. This is especially necessary for hand-dyed rugs that can be more sensitive to light exposure.

CLEANING

The goal of washing the rug, beyond keeping it clean, is to avoid accidentally felting the yarns, fading the colors, or causing the colors to bleed. Washing the rug by hand with mild, wool-friendly detergents and cold water will reduce the likelihood of all three undesired outcomes. Do a test of your cleaning materials on the underside of the rug before washing the whole thing.

Spot Clean

If you just need to clean a small part of the rug, there's no need to do a full wash. Again, start by testing a small area on the underside of the rug before working on a more visible area. Spot clean by patting the area firmly with a clean, wet rag. Do not rub the fibers back and forth. Continue until the spot is thoroughly wet. Rinse the area with cold water and lay flat to dry.

Full Wash

If you need to wash the entire rug, submerge it in cold water and allow it to soak for one hour. Agitate the rug gently, and if necessary, use a mild, wool-friendly soap. Avoid products containing bleaches or heavy detergents. Products such as Woolite or Eucalan No Rinse Delicate Wash work well.

Refresh the water and repeat the process with more soap if necessary. Rinse the rug. Do not wring or twist the water out. Pressing on it while you rinse it will help release any dirt buildup. Repeat this process until the water runs clear.

After pressing as much water out of the rug as possible without wringing or twisting, roll the rug up, loops facing out, in several fluffy towels, and apply weight or pressure to allow the towels to absorb some of the water. Finally, lay it flat to dry.

Machine Wash

I'll admit that many punched rugs (made with rug yarn) can handle a gentle wash cycle—I've done it myself with good results—but it's a gamble that could easily lead to stretching, felting, color bleeding, or lost loops. Some yarns are more resilient than others to this method, and it's hard to know without risking your piece. Machine wash at your own risk, and always with cold water. Lay flat to dry.

Cleaning with Snow

If you live in an area that receives snow, take your rug outdoors and pile fresh snow on top of it with a broom. Then vigorously sweep the snow away. Dry snow in very cold temperatures works best; it sits on the surface of the rug rather than penetrating it deeply. Repeat as many times as desired. This method lightly cleans the surface of the rug without soaking it. The sweeping action can increase the halo of fuzz on the rug, so you may need to give it a once-over with a lint remover or lint shaver.

DYEING WOOL YARNS

Dyeing yarn might sound daunting at first, but in practice, it's quite simple and can actually be intuitive. My best advice? Build color gradually to allow yourself the room to experiment and fine-tune your hues as you go.

I use acid dyes to immersion dye yarn, completely submerging the yarn in water with the dye to create an easy and even distribution of color. For a consistent color distribution, stir the yarn frequently as the dye sets. If you want a more varied and tonal effect instead of a solid color, play with pouring the dye stock strategically onto parts of the yarn and stir less frequently. There is a lot of room for testing and play!

If you want to produce exact and consistent color results, measure the dye powders with a jewelry scale or a digital kitchen scale, and take good notes to document your results. You might even want to snip and keep a piece of yarn to have as a record of each color to go along with your notes. My process is not very exact; I prefer to experiment with color, often without the use of a scale. But taking notes is never a bad thing!

These instructions are meant for protein fibers: wool, fur, silk. So dye-friendly cellulose fibers, like cotton or linen, will yield different results. As always, wool rug yarns are my favorite for dyeing, as they are resilient and unlikely to felt.

All of the projects in this book use yarn I've dyed myself. I use PRO Washfast Acid Dyes for all my colors. See Resources (page 142) for more on sourcing dyes.

golden ocher yarn

MATERIALS AND TOOLS

Off-white unbleached wool rug yarn or other protein fiber yarn

Yarn ties

1–2 bowls or tubs

Measuring cups and spoons

Synthrapol detergent

Dye pot

Citric acid or white vinegar

Stovetop or other heat source

Glass jar or container

PRO Chemical Acid Dyes in: WF Sun Yellow 119, WF Golden Yellow 199c, WF Grasshopper 719, WF Chestnut 560, or other acid dyes

Small spoons or mixing stick

Tongs

Liquid dish soap

notes on materials

Yarn ties are used to hold the yarn into skeins, and can be made of any material that won't leach color, like undyed yarn or string. Feel free to choose any color dye for your projects, and see Resources (page 142) for additional recommended brands of acid dyes. Synthrapol detergent is specifically made for dyeing processes. Finish Jet-dry is a similar product that works great, and Dharma Trading Co. also carries their own version of synthrapol detergent. Make sure the yarn is in a skein, not wound into a ball, or the dye will not evenly color all the yarn. Choose aluminum or stainless steel for the dye pot, as non-enameled and copper pots are reactive and can affect the color of the dyes. White enamel pots (without any chips) can also work great.

note

Do not use any tools during the dyeing process that you also use for cooking. Keep all dyeing tools and materials separate.

Chemical and acid dyes should not be inhaled or ingested. So it's a great idea to wear a dust mask while handling the dye powders, and to wear gloves through the process to prevent skin irritation. Keep a tidy workstation, and clean thoroughly after dyeing, as the dyes can easily discolor unprotected surfaces like countertops.

DYEING YARN

1 Lay out the skein of yarn. Use the yarn ties to loosely tie the bundles of yarn together so they don't tangle. Do not tie too tightly, or the dye will not be able to penetrate the yarn underneath the ties (though maybe experiment with how that might look!). *fig. A*

2 Submerge the yarn in a tub or bowl filled with warm water, and add Synthrapol detergent to the water. Use a rough ratio of 1 teaspoon per 2 quarts of water. Allow the yarn to soak for 30 minutes.

3 Move the yarn to the dye pot and cover it with water, making sure there is enough water for the yarn to move freely when you stir the pot. Add 1 tablespoon of citric acid or ¼ cup of vinegar. Heat to a simmer. Don't let it boil.

4 While the water heats, create a dye stock. Heat 1 cup of water (to around 180° F or 82° C) in a glass jar or container. Add dye powder to the water and stir until it is dissolved. Follow the manufacturer's instructions for water to powder ratio, and if you're in doubt, use less dye as a starting point. Add any dye colors or combinations of dye colors you desire. *figs. B-C*

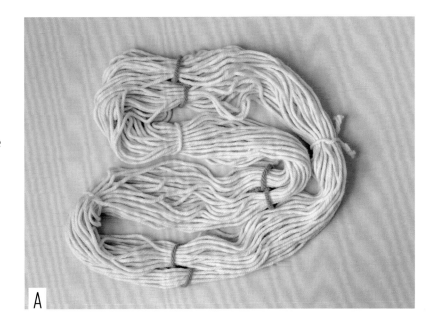

A

B

C

5 Add the dye stock to the pot. Immediately stir the yarn with tongs, dispersing the dye through the yarn and around the pot. Because the water is acidic, the dye will set quickly, so stir as you pour for the most uniform finish. *fig. D*

6 Allow the yarn to sit in the dye bath until all the color has been absorbed and the water is clear. Stir occasionally to ensure the dye doesn't settle to the bottom of the pot. Stir more often for the most uniform finish. Some dyes, depending on their color, take longer to set. When the water is clear, the dye bath has been *exhausted. fig. E*

D

E

7 Assess the color of the yarn. Decide if you're happy with it, or would like to adjust or increase the color saturation. Remember that the yarn will dry slightly lighter than it looks while it's wet.

If you want to add more color, create a new dye stock by repeating Step 4. Add it to the pot, repeating Steps 5 and 6. You may need to add additional citric acid or vinegar if the yarn is not taking up the color after an extended period of time. You can repeat this process until you achieve your desired color. *fig. F*

8 Prepare a tub or bowl of fresh water with a small squeeze of liquid dish soap. This will neutralize the vinegar or citric acid. Once you've achieved your desired color, remove the yarn and place it into the tub or bowl for a few minutes. Afterward, give the yarn a quick rinse under cool water to remove the soap residue. Gently squeeze as much water as possible from the yarn, and hang it to dry. *fig. G*

F

G

ON DESIGN AND COLOR

DESIGN YOUR OWN RUG

Near the turn of the twentieth century, if a rug hooker (punch needle or traditional) had the means, they would almost always purchase a preprinted pattern: a piece of burlap stamped with a rug design ready to be hooked. There were heaps of designs to choose from. Rug designers and businesses like Edward Sands Frost, Garrett's, and Pearl K McGown were all influential in their respective times, with their designs playing a large role in what rug makers were making. Really, their influence within the community is still felt today.

These predesigned hooked rugs are beautiful, but ask enthusiasts and collectors, and they will tell you that they often place the highest value on early rugs that do not use preprinted patterns. Rugs with original designs drawn by the individual artist are highly treasured, whether crafted with realistic motifs or a primitive style. They're valued for their originality.

Certainly, there's nothing wrong with using a pattern. Patterns are *such* great tools, and it can be a lot of fun finding a design that you connect with (while supporting a fellow punch needle artist!). But if you've got a creative itch that needs scratching, I encourage you to put your ideas on paper and design a rug that reflects you.

It might be helpful to know that hooked rugs are often classified depending on their style and subject. Stylistically, hooked rugs usually fall somewhere within the following three categories:

Primitive Hooking: Designs in this category often showcase simplistic, childlike forms characterized by large blocks of color. This style often forgoes realistic elements such as shadows and shading, favoring bold, graphic design elements instead. It might be considered more illustrative, and most designs in this book fall into this category.

Fine Hooking: Rugs in this category have designs that pay close attention to the definition of shapes. They capture the finer details of a scene or subject, often using shading and a realistic perspective to convey a sense of realism.

Abstract and Geometric Hooking: A geometric hooked rug often features designs that are based on geometric shapes—like squares, triangles, circles—often arranged in a repeating pattern. Abstract hooked rugs, on the other hand, utilize non-representational forms and color to create designs that do not depict a specific object or scene, instead focusing on form, overall composition, and expression. I often use these design elements as things like borders within my work.

In addition to the *style*, we also have the *subject* to think about. Hooked rugs are often classified by their subject. When looking at some of these standard subject categories, there are several groups to draw from: florals, animals, landscape, designs inspired by daily life, and again, geometric and abstract. Within these categories of style and subject, there are infinite possibilities when it comes to design, and many rugs are a combination of several categories. Additionally, you may go beyond these subjects to punch whatever your heart desires! But if you're feeling overwhelmed, start by narrowing your options. Select a style and a subject from the lists in this chapter. Choose something that resonates with you, and pull out a piece of paper to start sketching possible ideas.

I have always leaned toward designs that are primitive in style, sometimes with minimalism in mind. I like to choose a central motif and sketch it out using exaggerated shapes, drawn with a loose hand, in a quick and reflexive manner. Then I tend to go back and refine or adjust the shapes. I work until my subject *feels right*, which often requires taking a break when a drawing feels overworked or overstudied. Design is so subjective, but the throughline I like to follow is a sense of playfulness and simplicity. I usually forgo using any shading or fine detail. When there's enough room, or if the composition requires it, I'll add a frame around the border, or supportive decorative elements to highlight the subject, just as was often done with hooked rugs from the late nineteenth and early twentieth centuries.

PUNCH NEEDLE RUG HOOKING HANDBOOK

Because my designs are so simple, achieving balance in composition and color is essential. I make sure that the weight of my lines and shapes remains consistent throughout the design, and that elements are placed carefully so that there is an even distribution of weight across the piece. I try to achieve a sense of balance across the design. For example, when I drew the Mirrored Tulips Pillow (page 102) pattern, I made the leaves and stems thick-bodied and repetitive. This makes those elements (the leaves and stems) read as a single shape, making them weighty enough to counterbalance the exaggerated flower heads. To prevent the design from feeling cluttered, the background is just a solid color in a light, neutral hue, providing breathing room for the design.

On larger rugs, there's much more room for ornamental detail, although I usually like to keep the overall composition fairly simple. But when space allows, I like to build complexity to my designs by adding flowers or graphic/geometric borders using basic shapes. I draw without the help of a ruler so that my lines look more human and hand-drawn. I embrace my mistakes! These are my own design guidelines, and I encourage you to follow the leanings and styles that speak to your own aesthetic tastes.

ON COLOR

Color is one of the more important factors within your work. The colors you use express a lot. I use a lot of color, but I'm careful and specific in my approach to choosing them. I pay particular attention to the *value* and *saturation* of the colors I choose; instead of using pure hues, I strive to create color palettes that include a balance of *tints*, *shades*, and *tones*.

Value refers to the lightness or darkness of a color. The closer a color is to black, the darker the value, and the closer it is to white, the lighter the value. Understanding value is important for the three elements below.

Saturation refers to the intensity of a color. This can sometimes be thought of as the purity of a color; the closer it is to an original hue, the more saturated it is. The more white, black, or gray that is added to a color, the more desaturated it is.

Tint: A tint is formed by adding white to a hue, making its value lighter. Tints are softer and lighter variations of their original hues. For example, sky blue is a tint of primary blue. If you're shopping for yarn, these colors are usually regarded as pastels. They are colors that feel light and airy. When you dye yarn, you start with white (or off-white) as a base. So, you can easily achieve tints if you don't oversaturate the yarn with dye.

Shade: A shade is produced when you add black to a hue, making its value darker. Shades are often rich, deep colors. You might notice that I rarely (if ever) use a flat black color in my work, but I do use dark colors—shades—for contrast and linework. In the Seafaring Ship Floor Rug (page 94), I use a lot of shades: dark blues and dark grays. One of the hand-dyed colors is a mix of dark brown and dark gray, creating a shade that's close to black, but not as flat or intense. Using shades gives my designs softer finishes. In a store, a version of the color I dyed might be labeled as an *antique black* or *charcoal*.

Tone: Tones are created by adding gray (black *and* white—gray) to a hue, which desaturates it, resulting in a color that is less vivid or intense. I pay very careful attention to saturation in my designs. I lean toward creating palettes that feel colorful, but are still pulled back—in other words, not too intense or saturated. So whenever a color is too saturated, I add grays (and very often, browns for warmth), turning my pure hues into tones. When you're shopping for colors that have this feeling, look for hues that feel weathered or aged.

Choosing colors is really subjective, so take inspiration from works of art that you love, or from color palettes suggested by the color wheel. There isn't a one-size-fits-all formula for creating a palette you love. Sometimes a bit of tension is exciting in a composition too! I like to create tension by choosing colors that don't naturally complement one another and putting them together in small doses (for instance, red and purple).

After you have a design set, map out your colors by laying them together over a neutral background in a manner that mimics their placement in your design. Stand back and see how well they play together. Swap out different colors and experiment. You can also make digital or colored pencil/marker mock-ups on paper. Keep playing until you're happy with the colors!

INSPIRATION

The character, patina, and beauty found in early hooked rugs is unbeatable. I like to flip through books and magazines, visit museums, and scroll through online images of vintage and antique hooked rugs to gather inspiration on composition, color, and style. I also like to draw inspiration from quilts. I often see parallels in the two textile forms; they both originated from utilitarian origins and became art forms thanks to the artists that made them. Both historic and modern quilt blocks can spark ideas, especially if you're drawn toward geometric combinations.

I also love drawing inspiration from children's drawings, made in that very precious stage before self-consciousness, expectation, and comparison take over. Exaggeration and freedom from any sort of

realism is celebrated in children's work! Have a look through drawings made by children; it's the most refreshing way to reset your mind and heart.

DESIGN AND EMBRACING MISTAKES

My personal design philosophy embraces the wobbly lines and skewed shapes that inevitably characterize handmade pieces. While some might consider them mistakes, I think they're lovely. These little imperfections are our own personal signatures and reminders that we are human. Don't shy away from showcasing the unique handcrafted nature of your rugs; these irregularities tell a story about the process, and in my mind, striving to erase them can lessen the gap between our very special wares and their machine-made counterparts.

If you decide to design your own rugs, I hope you'll bring a little bit of this philosophy with you; design, draw, and make freely without the pressure of perfection. One stipulation? Take extra care in the foundational elements of construction so that your piece will last for generations to come. And have fun!

CALCULATING YARN AND BACKING AMOUNTS

To determine the amount of monks cloth you need for a project or design of your own, add 10″ to the length and width of the finished size you're aiming for unless you're using a stretcher bar frame (see Stretcher Bar Frames, page 26). If you're using a gripper type frame, you want 5″ of clearance on all sides so that there's plenty of cloth to stretch and fit the frame. Say, for instance, you've designed a rug that measures 18″ × 30″. In that case, cut a piece of monks cloth that measures 28″ × 40″.

Yarn amounts are also quite simple to calculate. When punching a ¼″ loop with bulky yarn, 1 oz. is equal to roughly 17 square inches of punching. So you need 1 ounce of yarn for every 17 square inches.

To visualize this, cut a 3″ × 6″ rectangle template from paper. You'll need 1 ounce of yarn to fill each space that size (with a small buffer for error included within the template). Count or calculate how many times the rectangle fits within the size of your design. If it fits eight times, you'll need a minimum of 8 oz. of yarn. I recommend always getting a little extra, just in case. You don't want to run out in the middle of a project, *especially* if you're using hand-dyed yarns with colors that are difficult to re-create.

projects

TEMPLATES

To access the patterns for these projects, scan this QR code or go to **tinyurl.com/11584-patterns-download**

Download the patterns at full size, or in the print-at-home format. If printing at home, tape together the pattern pieces before cutting them out.

ON THE PROJECTS

All the projects in this book have been crafted using Briggs & Little Super 4 Ply yarn in colors I hand-dyed myself. If you prefer not to dye your own colors, this same yarn can also be purchased in a variety of commercially dyed colors (see Resources, page 142). You can, of course, also use a different brand of bulky wool rug yarn.

The yarn colors listed for each project are meant to serve as descriptions for my hand-dyed colors and are not the names listed or created by the brand. Use them as guides for selecting your own yarns.

Please note that I also refer to every project as a *rug*. Though many of them go on to serve other purposes—as pillows, wall hangings, bags, and more—they all begin as punched rugs.

floral trivet

FINISHED SIZE: 9″ × 12″

This is a bite-size project to acquaint yourself with the complete process of punch needle rug hooking. This trivet can be worked up in an afternoon or two! You might use this as a wall hanging, or if you're using a heat resistant yarn like wool, this piece makes a lovely trivet to keep your tabletop safe from hot teapots and bubbling casserole dishes. Either way, it's sure to be a sunny addition to your home!

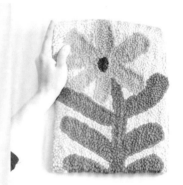

BACKING AND YARN

Monks cloth (12–14 holes per inch) with edges finished: 19″ × 22″

4 oz. bulky weight wool rug yarn in cream

3½ oz. bulky weight wool rug yarn in green

2½ oz. bulky weight wool rug yarn in golden yellow

½ oz. bulky weight wool rug yarn in brick red

TOOLS

Gripper strip frame and cover

Oxford Punch Needle, regular size 10

Black permanent marker

Scissors

Iron and towel

Hand-sewing needle and all-purpose thread

Paper

Masking tape

Fabric shaver or lint roller (optional)

Floral Trivet pattern (see Projects, page 68)

note

Remember, you can always use any of the punch needle or frame variations we reviewed in Tools and Materials (page 14)! Just make sure you're using a punch needle that punches ¼″ loops with bulky yarn. For more detailed information about each step, see Setting Up (page 30) and Punch Needle Rug Hooking Basics (page 34).

SETTING UP

1 Finish the edges of the backing (see Preparing the Backing, page 30). Transfer the pattern to the backing (see Transferring the Pattern, page 30). If you prefer, freehand the design onto the backing for your own personal touch.

2 Set the backing onto the frame with the design set in the middle. Tighten all sides of the backing onto the frame until the pattern is taut, but do not distort the design. Slip the cover over the frame.

PUNCHING

1 Using a border stitch (roughly 6 stitches per inch), punch the center circle of the flower with brick-red yarn, and fill it with the fill stitch (roughly 4 stitches per inch), spiraling inward from the border. After outlining and filling the center circle, snip the working end of the yarn ¼" above the backing, and push the tail through to the pile side of the project. If you prefer, leave the tail for now and push them all through once you've finished punching.

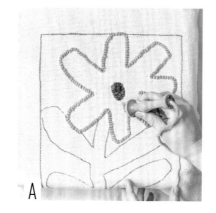

A

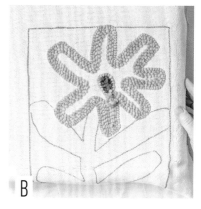

B

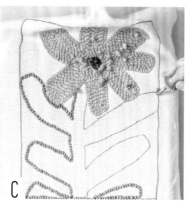

C

D

note

If, like me, you leave pushing through yarn tails until the end, you'll need to fill in any gaps that are left afterward with matching yarn. Ideally, punch no fewer than 3 stitches when filling gaps to ensure the stitches are secure.

E

2 Punch the outline of the flower head with golden-yellow yarn and border stitch. Where the flower petal meets the top of the trivet, add a second row of border stitches. Then fill the flower with the fill stitch, creating a brick-like pattern of staggered stitches. *figs. A-B*

3 Using a border stitch, punch the outline of the leaves and stem with green yarn. Add a second row of border stitches where the leaves and stem meet the base or sides of the trivet, reinforcing the exterior border. *fig. C*

4 Fill in the rest of the leaves and stem with a loose fill stitch. I worked from the outline of each leaf toward the stem. *fig. D*

5 Add two rows of border stitches in cream to the rectangular exterior of the trivet. Continue the border stitch around the entire exterior of the flower, leaves, and stem. Fill in the background with fill stitch. *fig. E*

note

Border and fill stitch lengths are great as general rules, but they are not always the *law*. Use your best judgment and increase your stitch length to add breathing room if an area of your project is becoming crowded or overpacked, especially in highly detailed designs. Most designs in this book are on the simple side, but this is good to keep in mind for future projects.

FINISHING

1 Carefully remove the project from the frame. If you have not done so already, push all yarn tails through the backing with a narrow pair of scissors, or the punch needle. Punch any remaining gaps. Flip the piece over, pile side up, and cut the tails flush to the loop pile. *figs. F-G*

2 Tidy the loops by pushing them into place with the scissors or punch needle. Take your time to define the shapes (see Tidying Loops, page 42). *fig. H*

3 On a heatproof surface, lay a damp towel over the loop side of the trivet (facing up). Press the rug with the appropriate heat setting on the iron. If necessary, use this process to correct any shaping issues, pressing out any unwanted irregularities with steam and heat (see Blocking, page 43). Let dry in place. *fig. I*

4 Trim the monks cloth to a 2″ perimeter on all sides of the trivet. Hem the monks cloth to the stitch side of the trivet (see Hemming, page 44). If desired, shave the loop side of the trivet with a fabric shaver or lint roller for a smooth finish. *figs. J-K*

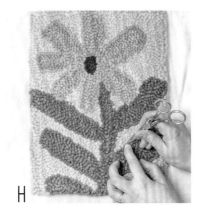

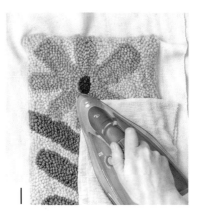

Folding the hem

Whipstitching the hem

bird in the garden floor rug

FINISHED SIZE: 19½″ × 26″

Imagine dedicating hours of your time, labor, and money to a project, only to trample on it regularly with shoes and feet. I mean, can you *really* use these projects as floor rugs? Yes! And you should! It's thrilling to see your pieces shine through humble daily use as you integrate them into your everyday life. It's like using your finest china, except on the floor, and with your feet.

The punch needle rug hooking process has been tested through generations of artists, so you can trust that these mats are resilient and can withstand regular use.

But remember two things:

1. The strength of the materials will affect the rug's longevity and performance.

2. Almost no rug is a match against an animal determined to claw away at it. Beware!

BACKING AND YARN

Monks cloth (12–14 holes per inch) with edges finished: 29½″ × 36″

20 oz. bulky weight wool rug yarn in off-white

8 oz. bulky weight wool rug yarn in purple

6 oz. bulky weight wool rug yarn in dark green

3 oz. bulky weight wool rug yarn in red

3 oz. bulky weight wool rug yarn in blue

3 oz. bulky weight wool rug yarn in green

3 oz. bulky weight wool rug yarn in yellow

3 oz. bulky weight wool rug yarn in purple

1 oz. bulky weight wool rug yarn in charcoal

TOOLS

Gripper strip frame and cover

Oxford Punch Needle, regular size 10

Black permanent marker

Scissors

Iron and towel

Hand-sewing needle and heavy-duty thread (upholstery or button and craft)

Paper

Masking tape

Fabric shaver or lint roller (optional)

Bird in the Garden pattern (see Projects, page 68)

note

Remember, you can always use any of the punch needle or frame variations we reviewed in Tools and Materials (page 14)! Just make sure you're using a punch needle that punches 1/4″ loops with bulky yarn. For this project, I recommend a gripper strip frame or similar so that tension can be adjusted while working. For more detailed information about each step, see Setting Up (page 30) and Punch Needle Rug Hooking Basics (page 34).

SETTING UP

1 Finish the edges of the backing (see Preparing the Backing, page 30). Transfer the pattern to the backing (see Transferring the Pattern, page 30). If you prefer, freehand the design onto the backing for your own personal touch.

2 Set the backing onto the frame with the bottom left corner of the design in the middle. Tighten all sides of the backing onto the frame until the pattern is taut, but do not distort the design. Slip the cover over the frame. As you work, move the project around on the frame, filling each area completely before moving on to the next (see Moving on a Gripper Strip Frame, page 41).

PUNCHING

1 Using a border stitch (roughly 6 stitches per inch), punch the outline of the bird's eye, beak, and the flower centers with charcoal yarn. Fill these areas with a fill stitch (roughly 4 stitches per inch). These areas, especially the bird's eye, will define the rug's personality.

note

It's easy to make the shapes of detailed elements like eyes too big or too small. Remember, you can adjust the stitch length and number of stitches you use to create your ideal shape. You can also always pull out stitches, adjust the backing, and try again. After you complete a detailed area, look at the loop side of the piece and determine if you need to make any adjustments.

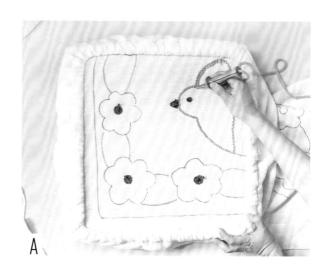

A

2 Border stitch the bird shape with purple. Outline the eye with purple. Fill in the bird that's accessible in the frame with a purple fill stitch. *fig. A*

TIP It's helpful to section large areas, like the bird's body or the background, into smaller, more manageable sections. Punch a smaller rough shape (anything will do!), and fill it in. Repeat until you've finished a whole area of a design.

3 Outline and fill the flowers and leaves with border and fill stitches. Use purple, red, and green for the bottom left flowers, as pictured. *fig. B*

B

4 Repeat Step 3 to outline and fill the leaves with dark green.

5 Punch two rows of border stitches around the perimeter of the rug with off-white. Punch one row of border stitches around the bird, flowers, and leaves. Then use fill stitches to fill the background, again dividing the area into smaller sections as needed. *fig. C*

Move the Rug on the Frame

1 Carefully remove the piece from the frame by pulling one end of the unpunched cloth *away* from the grippers and then *up* off the frame. This will release the tension. Once the tension has been released, roll or pull it in the opposite direction, toward the punched area, and carefully remove the piece from the frame. Removing the tension by releasing the monks cloth allows you to release the punched loops without damaging them. *fig. D*

2 Reposition the backing onto the frame with the top left corner of the design in the center. Stretch and secure onto the frame. Stabilize the punched part of the work that touches the needles with your hand to counteract the pulling while you tighten. Add the frame cover. *fig. E*

TIP When working on larger pieces like this one, steam pressing as you go will help keep the rug from curling away from the frame. When you remove the piece from the frame, you may want to steam it before putting it back on and continuing to punch.

C

D

Moving the piece on the frame later in the stitching process

E

CONTINUE PUNCHING

1 Punch the top left section of the rug, repeating Steps 3–5 in Punching (page 76). Punch the flowers in blue and yellow. Then border stitch and fill the background. *fig. F*

2 Move the rug to the top right section of the design. Outline and fill the flower centers in charcoal. Outline and fill the second half of the bird in purple. Outline and fill the leaves with dark green. *fig. G*

TIP To create a seamless transition when connecting two punched areas, avoid creating a cluster of cut tails. Connect shapes with abutting lines of stitches, distancing the cut tails from one another where possible.

3 Outline and fill the flowers in purple, red, and green as shown. Based on frame positioning, you may not be able to completely finish each flower. Border stitch and fill the background. *fig. H*

4 Move the rug on the frame as necessary to access any remaining unpunched sections. Trace and fill any remaining flowers and leaves. Border stitch the design elements with the off-white background color, and punch two rows of border stitches around any remaining perimeter of the rug. Fill the background, finishing the piece.

F

G

H

FINISHING

1 Carefully remove the project from the frame. If you have not done so already, push all yarn tails through the backing with a narrow pair of scissors, or the punch needle. Punch any remaining gaps. Flip the piece over and cut the tails flush to the loop pile.

2 Tidy the loops by pushing them into place with the scissors or punch needle. Take your time to define the shapes (see Tidying Loops, page 42).

3 On a heatproof surface, lay a damp towel over the loop side of the rug. Press the rug with the appropriate heat setting on the iron. If necessary, use this process to correct any shaping issues, pressing out any unwanted irregularities with steam and heat (see Blocking, page 43). Let dry in place.

4 Trim the monks cloth, allowing for a 3″ perimeter on all sides of the rug.

5 Hem the monks cloth to the stitch side of the rug (see Hemming, page 44) with heavy duty thread like upholstery or button and craft thread. If desired, shave the loop side of the rug with a fabric shaver or lint roller for a smooth finish.

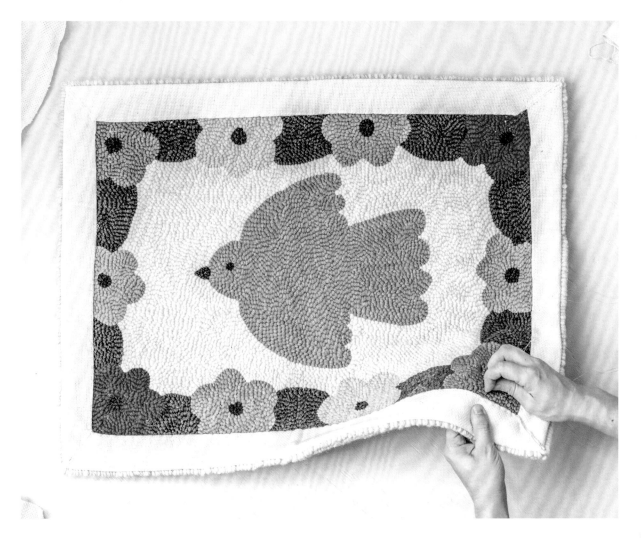

single bloom pillow

FINISHED SIZE: 15″ × 15″

I like to stuff pillows with the millions of little bits of yarn that accumulate from punching projects. I love bringing no-waste elements to my work, and if you're using wool scraps, they make a luxurious, antibacterial, and surprisingly hypoallergenic stuffing. If you don't have enough scraps on hand, give an old cushion new life by using it as a pillow insert, or of course you can use a more standard pillow stuffing.

The large blocky shapes in this design lend well to beginners or anyone wanting a speedy weekend project. Try it with your own color combination to suit your space!

BACKING AND YARN

Monks cloth (12–14 holes per inch) with edges finished: 25″ × 25″

Canvas or other heavy cotton fabric for pillow backing: 18″ × 18″

14 oz. bulky weight wool rug yarn in off-white

5½ oz. bulky weight wool rug yarn in blue

3 oz. bulky weight wool rug yarn in red

½ oz. bulky weight wool rug yarn in pink

Materials for stuffing (scraps, pillow insert, stuffing)

TOOLS

Gripper strip frame and cover

Oxford Punch Needle, regular size 10

Black permanent marker

Scissors

Iron and towel

Hand-sewing needle and all-purpose thread

Sewing pins

Paper

Masking tape

Fabric shaver or lint roller (optional)

Sewing machine (optional)

Serger (optional)

Pinking shears (optional)

Single Bloom pattern (see Projects, page 68)

note

Remember, you can always use any of the punch needle or frame variations we reviewed in Tools and Materials (page 14)! Just make sure you're using a punch needle that punches 1/4″ loops with bulky yarn. For more detailed information about each step, see Setting Up (page 30) and Punch Needle Rug Hooking Basics (page 34).

SETTING UP

1 Finish the edges of the punch needle backing (see Preparing the Backing, page 30). Transfer the pattern to the backing (see Transferring the Pattern, page 30). If you prefer, freehand the design onto the backing for your own personal touch.

2 Set the backing onto the frame with the flower part of the design set in the middle. Tighten all sides of the backing onto the frame until the pattern is taut, but do not distort the design. Slip the cover over the frame.

note

The simplicity of this design relies on crisp, clean lines, making this a great project for practicing rows of abutting border stitches.

PUNCHING

1 Using a border stitch (roughly 6 stitches per inch), punch the outline of the flower center with pink yarn. Fill in with a fill stitch (roughly 4 stitches per inch). Punch in a spiral. *fig. A*

A

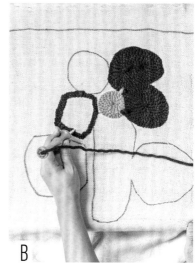

B

C

D

2 Outline the petals in red with a border stitch. Fill with a fill stitch. *fig. B*

3 Outline and fill the stem and leaves in blue. You may not be able to completely fill these shapes yet until you move the piece on the frame. *fig. C*

4 Punch two rows of border stitches around the perimeter of the pillow in off-white. Outline the flower, stem, and leaves in off-white. Fill stitch the background.

5 Move the piece on the frame to reach the rest of the design (see Moving on a Gripper Strip Frame, page 41). Repeat Steps 3 and 4 to outline and fill the rest of the stem, leaves, and background of the pillow. *fig. D*

FINISHING

1 Carefully remove the project from the frame. If you have not done so already, push all yarn tails through the backing with a narrow pair of scissors, or the punch needle. Punch in any remaining gaps. Flip the piece over and cut the tails flush to the loop pile. *fig. E*

2 Tidy the loops by pushing them into place with the scissors or punch needle. Take your time to define the shapes, especially on this simple pattern (see Tidying Loops, page 42).

3 On a heatproof surface, lay a damp towel over the loop side of the rug. Press the rug with the appropriate heat setting on the iron. If necessary, use this process to correct any shaping issues, pressing out any unwanted irregularities with steam and heat (see Blocking, page 43). Let dry in place.

E

PILLOW BACKING

1 Lay the 18″ × 18″ cotton pillow backing over the loop side of the piece. Pin together close to the punched edge, being careful not to pin down any loops of yarn. Leave a 6″ gap along the bottom of the pillow.

2 Sew the pillow backing and monks cloth together with a straight stitch, either using a backstitch by hand (page 51) or a sewing machine. Stitch as close to the loops as possible without sewing them down. Do not sew across the 6″ gap. *fig. G*

3 Cut away the excess monks cloth, leaving a 1½″ border (and if necessary, excess backing). If you'd like to finish the raw edges, do so with a zigzag stitch on a sewing machine, with a serger, or with pinking shears. *fig. F*

4 Turn the pillow cover right side out through the gap. Fill it with your choice of stuffing. Sew the 6″ gap closed by hand using a ladder stitch (page 50). If desired, shave the rug with a fabric shaver or lint roller for a smooth finish. *figs. H-I*

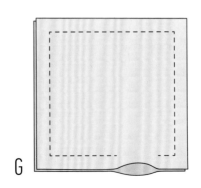

G

F

H

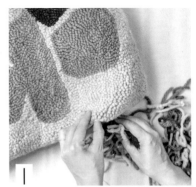

I

home sweet home doorstop

PROJECT SIZE: 9˝ × 8½˝ × 4˝

My family's house, built in the early 1930s, was never modernized with an open concept floor plan. Instead, we have many small rooms with an amazing number of doors, perfect for hiding away messy crafts and heaps of yarn. In my workspace alone, I can count six doorways. You may not have as many doors to contend with, but I'm sure you have a few—this friendly prop will hold one open with charm. If you prefer, you can also make this without a weight inside, creating a soft and light shelf sculpture!

BACKING AND YARN

Monks cloth (12–14 holes per inch) with edges finished: 28˝ × 30˝

11 oz. bulky weight wool rug yarn in off-white

6¼ oz. bulky weight wool rug yarn in red

2 oz. bulky weight wool rug yarn in sky blue

1¼ oz. bulky weight wool rug yarn in green

1 oz. bulky weight wool rug yarn in yellow

½ oz. bulky weight wool rug yarn in brown

¼ oz. bulky weight wool rug yarn in charcoal

TOOLS

Gripper strip frame and cover

Oxford Punch Needle, regular size 10

Black permanent marker

Scissors

Box cutter

Iron and towel

Hand-sewing needle and heavy-duty thread (upholstery or button and craft)

Sewing pins

Paper

Masking tape

Packing tape

Sturdy cardboard

Brick or suitably shaped rock/weight, smaller than 4˝ × 8½˝

Fabric shaver or lint roller (optional)

Sewing machine (optional)

Serger (optional)

Pinking shears (optional)

Home Sweet Home pattern (see Projects, page 68)

note

Remember, you can always use any of the punch needle or frame variations we reviewed in Tools and Materials (page 14)! Just make sure you're using a punch needle that punches 1/4˝ loops with bulky yarn. For this project, I recommend a gripper strip frame or similar so that tension can be adjusted while working. For more detailed information about each step, see Setting Up (page 30) and Punch Needle Rug Hooking Basics (page 34).

SETTING UP

1 Finish the edges of the backing (see Preparing the Backing, page 30). Transfer the pattern to the backing (see Transferring the Pattern, page 30). If you prefer, freehand the design onto the backing for your own personal touch.

2 Set the backing onto the frame with one part of the main house design set in the middle. Tighten all sides of the backing onto the frame until the pattern is taut, but do not distort the design. Slip the cover over the frame.

PUNCHING THE HOUSE

1 Start with the details. Using a border stitch (roughly 6 stitches per inch), punch in the window bars in brown. Punch in the doorknob with charcoal, using a minimum of 3 stitches. With a border stitch, trace the flower stems in green. *fig. A*

2 Border stitch the outline of the roof in red, then fill it with fill stitch. Repeat with the doorway in green and the windows in sky blue.

3 For this project, we'll be making larger loops for the flowers to give them a bolder texture. Thread the punch needle with yellow yarn. Punch down into the circle marking one flower. With the needle still in the backing, reach onto the loop side of the piece and pull on the yarn, lengthening the loop to about 1″ long (instead of ¼″). Pinch the yarn to hold it in place, then pull the needle up.

4 Repeat Step 3 to punch 5–6 stitches with long loops in each flower. The stitches should be dense (close to one another) and in a circular shape. *figs. B-C*

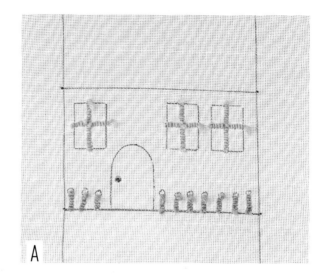

A

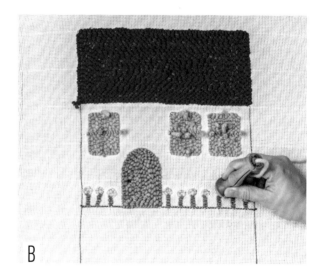

B

C

5 With off-white yarn, border stitch around the perimeter of the house, beneath the roofline, and around the doors and windows. Because many stitches are packed tightly for the flowers, there is risk of overpacking. So punch around the flowers with a looser fill stitch. Switch back to a border stitch where the bottom of the exterior wall meets the base of the house. Fill in the wall with a fill stitch. Punch one row of border stitches along the base of the house.

6 Move the piece on the frame to center the other side of the house (see Moving on a Gripper Strip Frame, page 41). Repeat Steps 1–5 to punch the other side of the house. Fill in the space between the houses with off-white.

7 Punch the 2 triangular wall pieces. Start with the flowers, punching the green stems and yellow 1″ loop petals. Outline and fill the roof with red. Outline and fill the wall with off-white. Only use one row of border stitches around the perimeter of each triangle instead of the standard two. *fig. D*

CONSTRUCTION

1 Carefully remove the project from the frame. If you have not done so already, push all yarn tails through the backing with a narrow pair of scissors, or the punch needle. Punch in any remaining gaps. Flip the piece over and cut the tails flush to the loop pile.

2 Tidy the loops by pushing them into place with the scissors or punch needle. Take your time to define the shapes (see Tidying Loops, page 42).

3 On a heatproof surface, lay a damp towel over the loop side of the rug. Press the rug with the appropriate heat setting on the iron. Work carefully around the flowers so you don't flatten them. If your iron doesn't have much maneuverability, wet the area between the flowers with hot water and apply pressure with another tool or your hands. If necessary, use this process to correct any shaping issues, pressing out any unwanted irregularities with steam and heat (see Blocking, page 43). Let dry in place.

4 Trim all pieces so there is 1½″ perimeter of monks cloth on all sides. If you'd like to finish the edges, do so with a zigzag stitch on a sewing machine, with a serger, or with pinking shears.

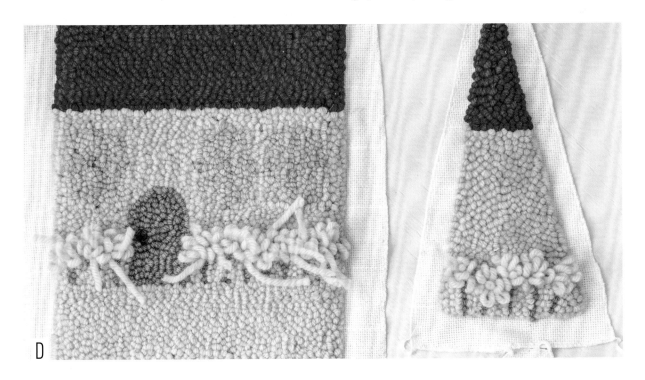

D

Shaping Flowers

1 From the loop side of the project, cut evenly across each cluster of yellow yarn with a sharp pair of scissors, keeping the loops about ¼" above the surrounding rug pile. If you prefer longer loops, cut less yarn away. Hold the bunch up lightly as you trim for even cutting.

2 Shape each flower into a round dome, cutting away yarn from the edges and separating neighboring blooms. Shape and round each puff until you're satisfied with the rounded, half-orb shape. *fig. E*

Cardboard Support with Weight

1 Use the paper pattern to trace and cut out the house shapes from the piece of cardboard. Make sure to mark the base of the house on each side of the rectangle. Cut slightly inside the lines, ensuring the piece will fit within the punch needle cover. *fig. F*

2 On a protected surface, use the box cutter or scissors to score the two lines that mark the base of the house on each side.

3 Place the brick or weight on the center of the house. With the scored baselines facing out, fold and tape the cardboard rooflines together. *figs. G-H*

4 Tape the triangular sides onto each end of the house form. *fig. I*

E

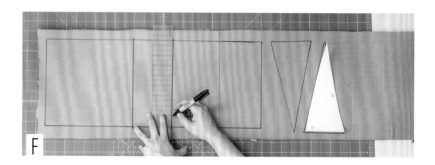

F

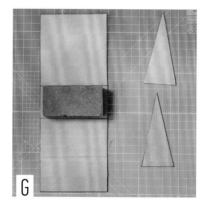

G

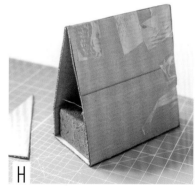

H

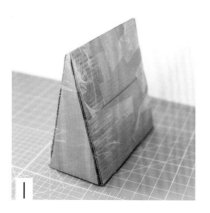

I

Final Assembly

1 Working with the finished punch needle pieces again, pin the base of the triangular sides to the base of the house, all stitch sides facing up. The seam allowances should be on the stitch side of the pieces. Sew the bottom of the triangle pieces to the main house by hand with a backstitch (page 51). Sew as close as possible to the loops. No backing should be visible from the loop side, so stitch into the loops slightly if necessary to achieve this. *fig. J*

2 Flip the piece over so the loop side is facing up. Fold the house up, and pin the roofline together. Sew together by hand with a backstitch (page 51), again as close to the loops as possible, and ensuring no backing shows from the loop side. *fig. K*

3 Turn the piece right side out with the loops facing out. Fold up one triangular side and pin to the main house, enclosing the monks cloth backing inside. Sew together along both vertical edges with a whipstitch (page 48), sewing into the backing past the loop line to hide the thread within the pile.

4 Slide the cardboard form and brick into the remaining opening on the punch needle house. Fold the final triangle up, and sew the remaining wall to the main house with a whipstitch (page 48), enclosing the cardboard form within the house. If desired, shave with a fabric shaver or lint roller for a smooth finish. *fig. L*

J

K

L

butterfly collar

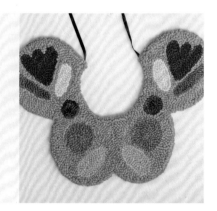

FINISHED SIZE: 13″ × 18″

The versatility of this collar makes it a dream to create and wear. It fits a great range of sizes from kids to adults, and is adaptable to wear over just about anything. Feel free to cut your own butterfly-inspired shapes to create a lively pattern and add a little flutter to your step.

BACKING AND YARN

Monks cloth (12–14 holes per inch) with edges finished: 24″ × 28″

Felt or wool fabric: 21″ × 17″

9¼ oz. bulky weight wool rug yarn in golden green/lime

2 oz. bulky weight wool rug yarn in red

1¼ oz. bulky weight wool rug yarn in blue

1¼ oz. bulky weight wool rug yarn in orange

1 oz. bulky weight wool rug yarn in green

1 oz. bulky weight wool rug yarn in off-white

1 oz. bulky weight wool rug yarn in charcoal

1 yd. of ¼″ wide ribbon in black

TOOLS

Gripper strip frame and cover

Oxford Punch Needle, regular size 10

Black permanent marker

Scissors

Rotary cutter (suggested)

Iron and towel

Hand-sewing needle and all-purpose thread

Thimble

Putty knife or disposable utensil for spreading glue

Roberts carpet adhesive

Paper

Masking tape

Fabric shaver or lint roller (optional)

Butterfly Collar pattern (see Projects, page 68)

note

Remember, you can always use any of the punch needle or frame variations we reviewed in Tools and Materials (page 14)! Just make sure you're using a punch needle that punches 1/4″ loops with bulky yarn. For more detailed information about each step, see Setting Up (page 30) and Punch Needle Rug Hooking Basics (page 34).

SETTING UP

1 Finish the edges of the backing (see Preparing the Backing, page 30). Transfer the pattern to the backing (see Transferring the Pattern, page 30). If you prefer, freehand the design onto the backing for your own personal touch. Play around with rearranging the shapes, or using different shapes than those that came in the pattern. Maintain symmetry to keep the collar reminiscent of butterfly wings. *fig. A*

2 Set the backing onto the frame with the design set in the middle as much as possible. Tighten all sides of the backing onto the frame until the pattern is taut, but do not distort the design. Slip the cover over the frame.

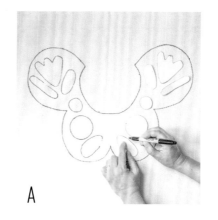
A

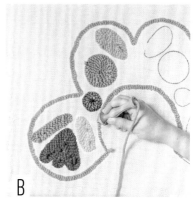
B

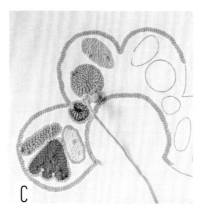
C

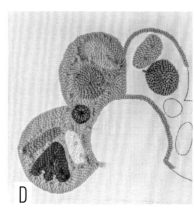
D

PUNCHING

1 Outline each shape within the collar with a border stitch (roughly 6 stitches per inch), and then use a fill stitch (roughly 4 stitches per inch) to fill each shape. Use green, red, off-white, charcoal, blue, and orange as shown, or select your own colors. Add two rows of border stitches around the entire collar in golden green/lime. *fig. B*

TIP Should you use one or two rows of border stitches? If a design element is small, detailed, or tightly stitched, opt for one row of border stitches to avoid overpacking. If a design is minimal or simple, use two rows: one in the color of the shape, and one in the abutting (often background) color. This helps to define a crisp line for each shape.

2 Outline the interior shapes with a border stitch in golden green/lime, and fill the background with the fill stitch. *figs. C-D*

3 Move the piece on the frame (see Moving on a Gripper Strip Frame, page 41). Repeat Steps 1 and 2 on the rest of the collar.

FINISHING

1 Carefully remove the project from the frame. If you have not done so already, push all yarn tails through the backing with a narrow pair of scissors, or the punch needle. Punch in any remaining gaps. Flip the piece over and cut the tails flush to the loop pile.

2 Tidy the loops by pushing them into place with the scissors or punch needle. Take your time to define the shapes (see Tidying Loops, page 42).

3 On a heatproof surface, lay a damp towel over the loop side of the rug. Press the rug with the appropriate heat setting on the iron. If necessary, use this process to correct any shaping issues, pressing out any unwanted irregularities with steam and heat (see Blocking, page 43). Let dry in place.

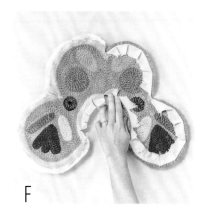

E

F

CONSTRUCTION

note

The adhesive used in this project is difficult to wash off of the tool you use to spread it. So use a dedicated tool like a putty knife or disposable utensil—not your favorite tool! Though you can use other glues, carpet adhesive is sturdy, water-resistant, and flexible. It also bonds nicely to wool and felt. Other glues may dry stiff, or flake and become brittle.

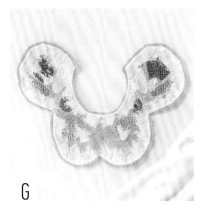

G

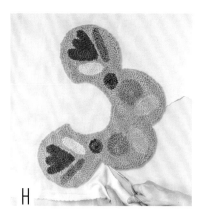

H

I

1 Spread a thin layer of Roberts carpet adhesive on the monks cloth around the collar on the stitch side, creating a ½″ border of glue. Leave to dry following the dry time instructions on the packaging. *fig. E*

2 When the adhesive is no longer tacky to the touch, cut away the excess monks cloth, leaving a 1″ border. Snip relief cuts into the glued monks cloth, making sure not to clip beyond the glue line. Fold the clipped tabs of fabric over onto the stitch side, and seal down with another layer of adhesive both above and below the fabric. Apply small dots of glue directly onto the yarn (stitch side) to firmly adhere the monks cloth and stabilize the backing. *figs. F-G*

3 With the adhesive still tacky, lay the collar, stitch and adhesive side down, over a similar-size piece of felt or wool fabric. Smooth the two layers together using your hands, pressing the glue into place.

4 Carefully cut away the excess wool or felt around the perimeter of the collar, using scissors or a small rotary blade. Let the adhesive dry completely. *fig. H*

5 Finish the edges by hand stitching a blanket stitch (page 51) around the entire perimeter of the collar through both layers. A thimble is helpful for pushing the needle through the layers. *fig. I*

6 Attach 15″ strips of ¼″ ribbon to each inner corner of the collar, hand sewing them down securely with several whipstitches (page 48). If desired, shave with a fabric shaver or lint roller for a smooth finish.

seafaring ship floor rug

FINISHED SIZE: 19″ × 25½″

Because I've spent my entire life in a maritime province, and now live in a neighborhood overlooking a harbor with tall ships, you might assume that I know a thing or two about the anatomy of a boat. I don't! But there is a lot of forgiveness in folk art, and despite the fact that I made up where all the sails and masts go, I still believe this ship to be seaworthy. It's a lucky schooner, I just know it.

BACKING AND YARN

Monks cloth (12–14 holes per inch) with edges finished: 29½″ × 36″

12½ oz. bulky weight wool rug yarn in light blue

10 oz. bulky weight wool rug yarn in red

6 oz. bulky weight wool rug yarn in off-white

4 oz. bulky weight wool rug yarn in medium blue

3 oz. bulky weight wool rug yarn in taupe

2 oz. bulky weight wool rug yarn in gold/mustard

2 oz. bulky weight wool rug yarn in charcoal

1¼ oz. bulky weight wool rug yarn in dark blue

TOOLS

Gripper strip frame and cover

Oxford Punch Needle, regular size 10

Black permanent marker

Scissors

Iron and towel

Hand-sewing needle and heavy-duty thread (upholstery or button and craft)

Sewing pins

Paper

Masking tape

Fabric shaver or lint roller (optional)

Seafaring Ship pattern (see Projects, page 68)

note

Remember, you can always use any of the punch needle or frame variations we reviewed in Tools and Materials (page 14)! Just make sure you're using a punch needle that punches 1/4″ loops with bulky yarn. For this project, I recommend a gripper strip frame or similar so that tension can be adjusted while working. For more detailed information about each step, see Setting Up (page 30) and Punch Needle Rug Hooking Basics (page 34).

SETTING UP

1 Finish the edges of the backing (see Preparing the Backing, page 30). Transfer the pattern to the backing (see Transferring the Pattern, page 30). If you prefer, freehand the design onto the backing for your own personal touch.

2 Set the backing onto the frame with the upper right part of the design in the middle. Tighten all sides of the backing onto the frame until the pattern is taut, but do not distort the design. Slip the cover over the frame.

note

The red blocks around the border in this design are slightly irregular for a playful, hand-drawn finish. If you prefer a more formal finish, cut a rectangular paper template and trace the rectangle around the border for more precision.

PUNCHING

1 Use a border stitch (roughly 6 stitches per inch) to outline the red blocks around the border of the design. Use two rows of border stitches where the blocks meet the perimeter of the rug. Border stitch the gold star. Border stitch the masts with the taupe yarn. Where they are thicker, fill them with a fill stitch (roughly 4 stitches per inch). Don't overpack areas with high densities of border stitches. *fig. A*

2 Fill the red rectangles and golden star with fill stitches. Border stitch the outer sail lines with off-white. If you reach a densely packed area, switch to fill stitch. Fill in the sail with fill stitch. Punch a light blue border stitch row below the sail. *fig. B*

3 Border stitch with light blue around the boat and between the sails and masts. Outline the red border blocks and gold star. Remember to switch to fill stitch in densely packed areas. Punch two rows of border stitches at the rug's perimeter. Outline and fill the hull with charcoal. Fill in the background with light blue. *fig. C*

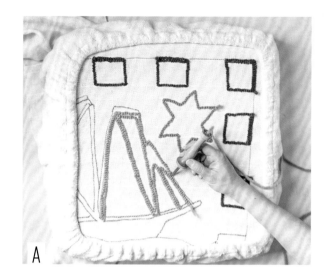

A

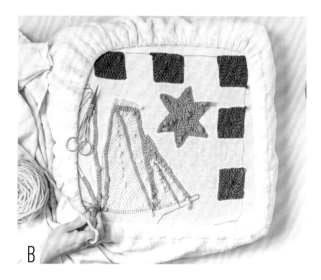

B

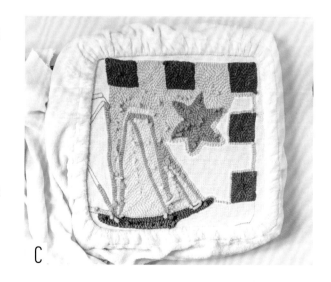

C

4 Move the piece on the frame (see Moving on a Gripper Strip Frame, page 41). Repeat Steps 1–3 to fill in the rest of the red border, sails, masts, hull, and golden sun along the top and left sides.

5 With the dark blue yarn, use border stitch to trace the interior wave lines. Move between one and two rows of stitching to create movement in the line width. Outline the surrounding water lines in medium blue. Fill the remaining water areas with medium-blue fill stitches. Include one row of light blue stitching between the bottom of the waves and the rug border. *figs. D-E*

6 Move the rug on the frame and repeat Steps 1–4 to finish punching all remaining areas of the rug. *fig. F*

FINISHING

1 Carefully remove the project from the frame. If you have not done so already, push all yarn tails through the backing with a narrow pair of scissors, or the punch needle. Punch in any remaining gaps. Flip the piece over and cut the tails flush to the loop pile.

2 Tidy the loops by pushing them into place with the scissors or punch needle. Take your time to define the shapes.

3 On a heatproof surface, lay a damp towel over the loop side of the rug. Press the rug with the appropriate heat setting on the iron. If necessary, use this process to correct any shaping issues, pressing out any unwanted irregularities with steam and heat (see Blocking, page 43). Let dry in place.

4 Trim the monks cloth to have a 3″ perimeter on all sides of the rug.

5 Hem the monks cloth to the stitch side of the rug (see Hemming, page 44) with heavy-duty thread. If desired, shave the rug with a fabric shaver or lint roller for a smooth finish. *fig. G*

D

E

F

G

framed flowers wall hanging

FINISHED SIZE: 14″ × 20″

PUNCHED AREA SIZE: 10½″ × 16½″

The benefits of using a canvas stretcher bar as a punch needle frame are twofold: You've got yourself an inexpensive way of getting into the craft, and the frame can act as a display frame.

Set the frame on your lap or lean it against a table as you work to ensure that you can punch the needle down fully into the backing without any obstructions.

This design also uses the stitch side as the display side. So the length of the stitches (border vs. fill stitches) is less important. Still make sure not to overpack the design, but put your main focus on creating neat and consistent stitches.

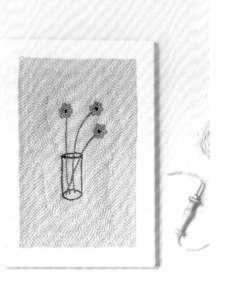

BACKING AND YARN

Monks cloth (12–14 holes per inch) with edges finished: 16½″ × 22½″

11¼ oz. bulky weight wool rug yarn in off-white

1 oz. bulky weight wool rug yarn in blue

¼ oz. bulky weight wool rug yarn in green

¼ oz. bulky weight wool rug yarn in charcoal

TOOLS

Canvas stretcher bar frame, 14″ × 20″

Oxford Punch Needle, regular size 10

Black permanent marker

Scissors

Iron and towel

Staple gun and staples

Paper

Masking tape

Framed Flowers pattern (see Projects, page 68)

note

Remember, you can always use any of the punch needle variations we reviewed in Tools and Materials (page 14)! Just make sure you're using a punch needle that punches 1/4″ loops with bulky yarn. This project specifically uses a stretcher bar frame for display purposes. For more detailed information about each step, see Setting Up (page 30) and Punch Needle Rug Hooking Basics (page 34).

SETTING UP

1 Finish the edges of the backing (see Preparing the Backing, page 30). Transfer the pattern to the backing (see Transferring the Pattern, page 30). If you prefer, freehand the design onto the backing for your own personal touch. You do not need to outline the border/perimeter.

2 See Stretcher Bar Frames (page 26) to set up the backing on the frame.

PUNCHING

1 Punch the center of each flower with charcoal yarn, using 3 stitches per flower center. *fig. A*

TIP For this project, push in your tails as you go. Since the stitch side will be displayed, you want to avoid inconsistencies in the stitch lines as much as possible.

2 Punch the flower heads in blue, following the contour of the flower shape closely to define the petals. *fig. B*

3 Punch the foreground of the vase in charcoal. Then punch the green stems. Finally, punch the rest of the vase between and behind the stems. *figs. C-D*

A

B

C

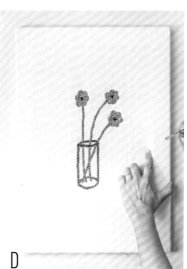

D

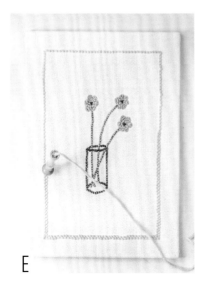

E

F

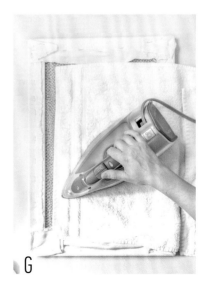

G

4 Use your finger to locate the wooden edge of the frame. Using that border as your guide, punch along the perimeter of the project with two rows of border stitch (roughly 6 stitches per inch) in off-white. *fig. E*

5 Fill in the background. Punch it in sections, creating rough shapes and then filling them in. Fill the interior of the vase as well. *fig. F*

FINISHING

1 Turn the piece over to the pile side. Trim all tails flush to the pile.

2 On a heatproof surface, lay a damp towel over the loop side of the piece. Press the piece with the appropriate heat setting on the iron. Let dry in place. *fig. G*

mirrored tulips pillow

FINISHED SIZE: 18″ × 18″

Some might say that pairing red and green brings to mind December decorating, but lately I've been craving this combination in all seasons and sneaking it into designs wherever I can. If you're not sure about pairing them yourself, here's an easy place to start; red flowers and green stems are an obvious fit, and the color wheel agrees—they're complementary!

BACKING AND YARN

Monks cloth (12–14 holes per inch) with edges finished: 28″ × 28″

2 pieces of canvas / heavy cotton fabric for envelope backing: 23″ × 17″ each

16 oz. bulky weight wool rug yarn in pink

9½ oz. bulky weight wool rug ply yarn in green

4 oz. bulky weight wool rug yarn in red

TOOLS

Gripper strip frame and cover

Oxford Punch Needle, regular size 10

Black permanent marker

Scissors

Iron and towel

Hand-sewing needle and all-purpose thread

Sewing pins

Paper

Masking tape

Pillow insert (20″ × 20″)

Sewing machine and zipper foot (optional)

Serger, pinking shears (optional)

Fabric shaver or lint roller (optional)

Mirrored Tulips pattern (see Projects, page 68)

note

Remember, you can always use any of the needle or frame variations we reviewed in Tools and Materials (page 14)! But for this project, I recommend a gripper strip frame or similar so that tension can be adjusted while working. The size of this piece is right on the border of what you can comfortably make on a stretcher bar frame (the larger the piece, the more likely it is to lose tension while working) and a piece this size is unlikely to fit easily within a hoop frame.

Make sure you're using a needle that punches 1/4″ loops with bulky yarn. For more detailed information about each step, see Setting Up (page 30) and Punch Needle Rug Hooking Basics (page 34).

SETTING UP

1 Finish the edges of the punch needle backing (see Preparing the Backing, page 30). Transfer the pattern to the backing (see Transferring the Pattern, page 30). If you prefer, freehand the design onto the backing for your own personal touch.

2 Set the backing onto the frame with the design set in the middle. Tighten all sides of the backing onto the frame until the pattern is taut, but do not distort the design. Slip the cover over the frame.

PUNCHING

1 Trace the flowers with a border stitch (6 stitches per inch) in red yarn. Then fill the flowers with fill stitches (4 stitches per inch) by punching sections in a spiral. Punch as much of the design as you can without moving the piece on the frame. *fig. A*

TIP Filling shapes in a spiral punching pattern isn't the only way to fill, but it can help ensure you won't end up with a cluster of yarn tails in any one spot.

2 Repeat Step 1 to trace and fill the stems and leaves with green yarn. Punch as much of the design as you can without moving the piece on the frame. *fig. B*

3 With pink yarn, punch two rows of border stitches along the perimeter of the frame. Then, continuing in a border stitch with the pink yarn, outline the flowers, stems, and leaves. Fill the remaining background space (without moving the piece on the frame) by sectioning the large spaces and filling them in. *figs. C-D*

A

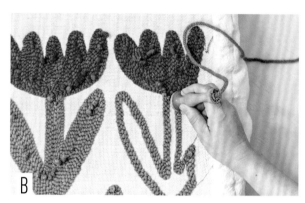

B

C

D

4 Move the piece on the frame (see Moving on a Gripper Strip Frame, page 41), then repeat Steps 1–3 to fill in the rest of the flower, stems, leaves, and background. *figs. E-G*

FINISHING

1 Carefully remove the project from the frame. If you have not done so already, push all yarn tails through the backing with a narrow pair of scissors, or the punch needle. Punch in any remaining gaps. Flip the piece over and cut the tails flush to the loop pile.

2 Tidy the loops by pushing them into place with the scissors or punch needle. Take your time to define the shapes (see Tidying Loops, page 42). *fig. H*

3 On a heatproof surface, lay a damp towel over the loop side of the rug. Press the rug with the appropriate heat setting on the iron. If necessary, use this process to correct any shaping issues, pressing out any unwanted irregularities with steam and heat (see Blocking, page 43). Let dry in place.

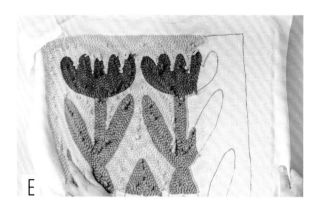

E

F

G

H

Envelope Pillow Backing

1 Press the backing fabric to remove any creases. Hem one 17″ edge on each backing piece by folding the edge to the wrong side 1″, pressing, folding another 1″, and then sewing down by hand or machine.

2 Trim the monks cloth around the punched piece, leaving a 2½″ perimeter on all sides. Lay the loop side of the pillow faceup, with the design oriented as you would display the pillow (flowers at the top). Lay the hemmed backing pieces on top of the pillow, right sides facing down. The first backing piece should cover the upper half of the pillow. The second backing piece should overlap the first backing piece and cover the lower half of the pillow. The two backing pieces should overlap by 7″ in the center, as shown. Pin the backing to the monks cloth of the pillow as close to the edge of the pile as possible (without pinning down any yarn). *fig. I*

3 Stitch around the entire perimeter of the pillow, securing the backing to the pillow front as close to the edge of the pile as possible, being mindful not to sew over any yarn. Stitch with a backstitch (page 51) by hand or by machine (using the zipper foot to get close to the edge). *fig. J*

I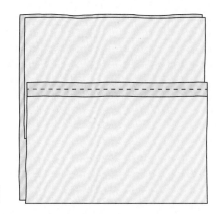

J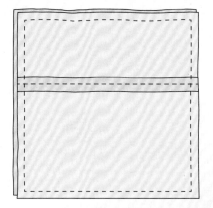

4 If desired, finish the raw seam allowance with a zigzag stitch, pinking shears, or serger.

5 Turn the pillow right side out. Add the pillow insert. If desired, shave the pile with a fabric shaver or lint roller for a smooth finish. *figs. K-L*

K

Turning right side out

L

playmates floor mat

FINISHED SIZE: 19½″ × 26″

Walking a lion by leash probably isn't the most sensible idea—look at those claws!—but I trust this young lady knows what she's doing. This design would be lovely in a variety of colors, so feel free to personalize the background and the figure to represent the adventurous spirit in your life.

BACKING AND YARN

Monks cloth (12–14 holes per inch) with edges finished: 29½″ × 36″

22 oz. bulky weight wool rug yarn in pale green

7 oz. bulky weight wool rug yarn in dark brown

6 oz. bulky weight wool rug yarn in yellow

3 oz. bulky weight wool rug yarn in dark orange

1 oz. bulky weight wool rug yarn in ivory

¼ oz. bulky weight wool rug yarn in dark taupe

TOOLS

Gripper strip frame and cover

Oxford Punch Needle, regular size 10

Black permanent marker

Scissors

Iron and towel

Paper

Masking tape

Hand-sewing needle and heavy-duty thread (upholstery or button and craft)

Paper

Fabric shaver or lint roller (optional)

Playmates pattern (see Projects, page 68)

note

Remember, you can always use any of the punch needle or frame variations we reviewed in Tools and Materials (page 14)! Just make sure you're using a punch needle that punches 1/4″ loops with bulky yarn. For this project, I recommend a gripper strip frame or similar so that tension can be adjusted while working. For more detailed information about each step, see Setting Up (page 30) and Punch Needle Rug Hooking Basics (page 34).

SETTING UP

1 Finish the edges of the backing (see Preparing the Backing, page 30). Transfer the pattern to the backing (see Transferring the Pattern, page 30). If you prefer, freehand the design onto the backing for your own personal touch.

2 Set the backing onto the frame with the top right part of the design set in the middle. Tighten all sides of the backing onto the frame until the pattern is taut, but do not distort the design. Slip the cover over the frame.

PUNCHING

Lion

1 Trace the lion's body with a border stitch (6 stitches per inch) in yellow. Fill the body with the same color and fill stitches (4 stitches per inch). Punch as much of the design as you can without moving the piece on the frame.

2 Using dark brown yarn, punch the lion's eyes, nose, and mouth with a tight border stitch. Use 4–5 tight stitches in a circle for each eye, and 4–5 stitches for the curve of the mouth.

3 Outline and fill the border polka dots with the same dark brown yarn.

4 Trace the lion's head (not the mane) using yellow and border stitch. Then border stitch around the eyes, nose, and mouth. Fill the rest of the lion's face. *fig. A*

5 Outline and fill the mane and tail with dark orange.

6 Punch two rows of border stitches in pale green along the perimeter of the rug. Outline all the design elements with the same border stitches. Fill the remaining background without moving the piece on the frame. *figs. B-C*

A

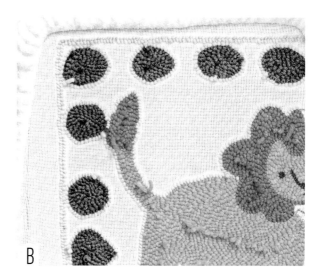

B

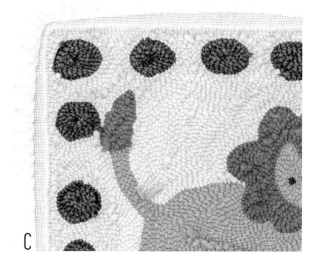

C

STEAM PRESS Since this is a larger project, steam press as necessary if your rug starts to curl away from the grippers and becomes difficult to manage. Remove the rug from the frame, then press the rug with a damp towel and hot iron to relax the loops, making the rug less unruly and easier to work with as it grows. See Blocking (page 43) for more details. Place the rug back on the frame (in this case, with the top left corner of the rug in the middle).

D

Girl

1 Move the rug on the frame, centering the top left corner (see Moving on a Gripper Strip Frame, page 41). With dark brown, punch 2 circles of 4–5 tight stitches for each eye.

2 While still using the dark brown yarn, outline and fill the leash, the polka dot border, and the girl's hair tie.

3 With the ivory, trace the face shape and around the eyes with a border stitch. Fill the girl's face. The eyes will determine the girl's expression, so feel free to turn the frame around once the surrounding areas have been punched and assess whether the eyes need an adjustment in stitch number or placement. Use the scissors to tidy the loops around her face before deciding. *fig. D*

E

4 Outline and fill the girl's hair with dark orange and arms with ivory. *fig. E*

5 Outline the dress with yellow and the sleeves with dark taupe. Punch two rows of border stitches in pale green along the perimeter of the rug. Outline all the design elements with the same border stitches. Fill the remaining background without moving the piece on the frame. *fig. F*

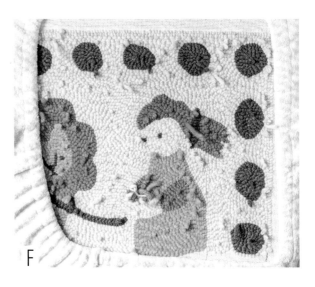
F

Bottom of the Rug

Move the piece on the frame as needed to fill in the bottom sections of the rug, starting with the bottom left corner, and then moving to the bottom right.

1 Punch the lion's claws in a dark brown border stitch. Punch some with two rows, and some with one row, varying their width. Outline and fill the lion's legs, and the polka dot border shapes with the same colors from the previous section. Border stitch all elements with the pale green, including two rows of border stitches at the rug's perimeter, and fill in the background. *fig. G*

2 Outline and fill the girl's legs with ivory and shoes with dark orange. Outline and fill the rest of the polka dot border with dark brown. Punch two rows of border stitches in pale green along the bottom perimeter of the rug. Outline all the design elements with the same border stitches. Fill the remaining background. *fig. H*

FINISHING

1 Carefully remove the project from the frame. If you have not done so already, push all yarn tails through the backing with a narrow pair of scissors, or the punch needle. Punch in any remaining gaps. Flip the piece over and cut the tails flush to the loop pile.

2 Tidy the loops by pushing them into place with the scissors or punch needle. Take your time to define the shapes (see Tidying Loops, page 42).

3 On a heatproof surface, lay a damp towel over the loop side of the rug. Press the rug with the appropriate heat setting on the iron. If necessary, use this process to correct any shaping issues, pressing out any unwanted irregularities with steam and heat (see Blocking, page 43). Let dry in place.

4 Trim the monks cloth, allowing for a 3˝ perimeter on all sides of the rug.

5 Hem the monks cloth to the stitch side of the rug (see Hemming, page 44) with a heavy-duty thread. If desired, shave the rug with a fabric shaver or lint roller for a smooth finish.

G

H

TIP Nonslip rug pads are a great addition to any handmade floor rug. No need to sew it to the rug—in fact, it's better not to for cleaning purposes. Simply place the hooked rug on top of the pad.

floral trio handbag

FINISHED SIZE: 12″ × 13.5″

This project is an excellent way to showcase your hard work and creativity. Accessorizing with this tote adds texture and interest to an outfit, all while giving you a soft place to store everyday essentials.

BACKING AND YARN

Monks cloth (12–14 holes per inch) with edges finished: 22″ × 37″

14 oz. bulky weight wool rug yarn in off-white

6 oz. bulky weight wool rug yarn in green

1¼ oz. bulky weight wool rug yarn in red

¼ oz. bulky weight wool rug yarn in yellow

TOOLS

Gripper strip frame and cover

Oxford Punch Needle, regular size 10

Black permanent marker

Scissors

Iron and towel

Masking tape

Hand-sewing needle and all-purpose thread

Thimble

Tapestry/yarn needle

Paper

1″ wide twill tape or rug binding: 30″

Putty knife or disposable utensil for spreading glue

Roberts carpet adhesive

Sewing pins (optional)

Fabric shaver or lint roller (optional)

Floral Trio pattern (see Projects, page 68)

note

Remember, you can always use any of the punch needle or frame variations we reviewed in Tools and Materials (page 14)! Just make sure you're using a punch needle that punches 1/4″ loops with bulky yarn. For this project, I recommend a gripper strip frame or similar so that tension can be adjusted while working. For more detailed information about each step, see Setting Up (page 30) and Punch Needle Rug Hooking Basics (page 34).

SETTING UP

1 Finish the edges of the backing (see Preparing the Backing, page 30). Transfer the pattern to the backing (see Transferring the Pattern, page 30). If you prefer, freehand the design onto the backing for your own personal touch.

2 Set the backing onto the frame with one side of the bag design set in the middle. Tighten all sides of the backing onto the frame until the pattern is taut, but do not distort the design. Slip the cover over the frame.

PUNCHING

1 Outline the center of the three flowers with yellow border stitches (6 stitches per inch). Fill the flower centers with fill stitches (4 stitches per inch). *fig. A*

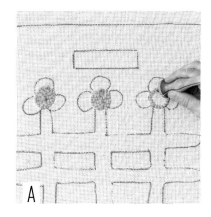
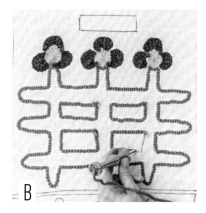
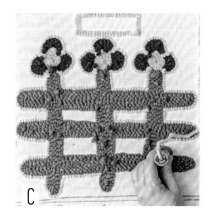
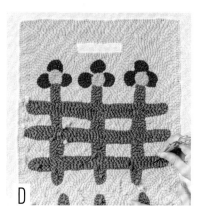

2 Outline the flower petals and centers with red border stitch. Fill the red petals. Outline the stems and leaves with green border stitch, then fill them. *fig. B*

3 Punch two rows of border stitch around the perimeter of the purse with off-white. Punch two rows around the handle. Outline around the floral elements, including the negative space between the leaves/stems, using one row of border stitches. *fig. C*

4 Fill the remaining background space in off-white.

5 Move the project on the frame (see Moving on a Gripper Strip Frame, page 41) and repeat Steps 1–4 to punch the other side of the bag. Fill in all the background.

FINISHING AND CONSTRUCTION

1 Carefully remove the project from the frame. If you have not done so already, push all yarn tails through the backing with a narrow pair of scissors, or the punch needle. Punch in any remaining gaps. Flip the piece over and cut the tails flush to the loop pile.

2 Tidy the loops by pushing them into place with the scissors or punch needle. Take your time to define the shapes (see Tidying Loops, page 42). *fig. D*

3 On a heatproof surface, lay a damp towel over the loop side of the rug. Press the rug with the appropriate heat setting on the iron. If necessary, use this process to correct any shaping issues, pressing out any unwanted irregularities with steam and heat (see Blocking, page 43). Let dry in place.

4 On the stitch side, spread a thin amount of carpet adhesive over the monks cloth inside the handle and onto the first few rows of yarn. Let the glue dry. *fig. E*

5 Cut an opening and relief clips within the handle (as pictured), making sure not to cut beyond the glue. *fig. F*

6 Fold cut tabs to the stitch side of the monks cloth, forming the handle opening. Seal the cut tabs down against the loops using a thin layer of carpet adhesive under each tab. Fold tightly so the tabs are not visible from the loop side.

7 Sew a 15″ length of twill tape or rug binding over the cut tabs on the stitch side, reinforcing it: First, lay the twill tape or rug binding around the handle opening, as shown, pinning if necessary. *fig. G*

8 Whipstitch (page 48) the interior and exterior borders of the twill tape, including the folds, stitching it directly into the monks

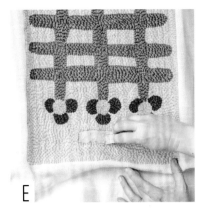

E

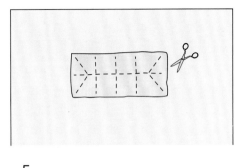

F

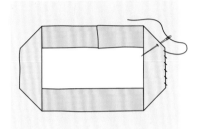

G

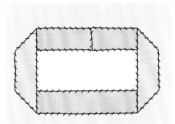

H

I

J

cloth. A thimble may be helpful to push the needle through. Repeat Steps 4–8 for the second handle. *fig. H*

9 Cut the monks cloth to a perimeter of 2″ around the entire purse. Hem the perimeter of the purse (see Hemming, page 44). *fig. I*

10 With the loop side facing out, fold the purse in half, matching the handles. With the yarn needle and off-white yarn, sew both sides together with a whipstitch (page 48). The hand stitching should sit directly next to the yarn loops on both sides, leaving no monks cloth visible. Start at the top of the purse, and stitch down to the base. After stitching, thread a 2½″ tail back up into the line of stitching to secure it. *fig. J*

11 Shave the handbag with a fabric shaver or lint roller for a smooth finish if desired.

cornflower scalloped floor rug

FINISHED SIZE: 23″ × 45″

Years before I started making them, I remember wanting hand-hooked rugs scattered everywhere around our home—floors, walls, stairs—anywhere! I wanted to make an entire collection for myself, but I had a nagging thought that the process was likely beyond my abilities, so the supplies I'd collected sat untouched for years.

I'm on the other side of that doubt now, and I invite you to join me. Can *you* make a large rug? Absolutely. It's easy. And guess what? There is no need for specialized equipment; you really don't need an extra-large, rug-size frame. With some patience, a rug of this size (and larger) can easily be made on a standard gripper strip frame. I do it often!

BACKING AND YARN

Monks cloth (12–14 holes per inch) with edges finished: 33″ × 55″

45 oz. bulky weight wool rug yarn in medium blue

21 oz. bulky weight wool rug yarn in pale blue

9 oz. bulky weight wool rug yarn in dark blue

7 oz. bulky weight wool rug yarn in off-white

TOOLS

Gripper strip frame and cover

Oxford Punch Needle, regular size 10

Black permanent marker

Scissors

Hand-sewing needle and heavy-duty thread (upholstery or button and craft)

Iron and towel

Paper

Masking tape

Fabric shaver or lint roller (optional)

Cornflower Scalloped pattern (see Projects, page 68)

note

Remember, you can always use any of the punch needle variations we reviewed in Tools and Materials (page 14)! Just make sure you're using a needle that punches 1/4″ loops with bulky yarn. For this project, I recommend a gripper strip frame or similar so that tension can be adjusted while working. For more detailed information about each step, see Setting Up (page 30) and Punch Needle Rug Hooking Basics (page 34).

SETTING UP

1 Finish the edges of the backing (see Preparing the Backing, page 30). Transfer the pattern to the backing (see Transferring the Pattern, page 30). If you prefer, freehand the design onto the backing for your own personal touch.

2 Set the backing onto the frame with the upper right part of the design in the middle. For a rectangle rug, I find it easiest to work from end to end instead of starting in the middle and working outward. Tighten all sides of the backing onto the frame until the pattern is taut, but do not distort the design. Slip the cover over the frame.

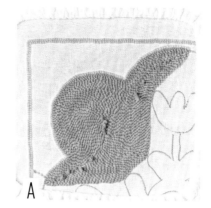

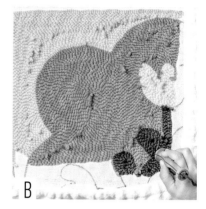

PUNCHING

Fill an entire section before moving the piece on the frame. Then move as necessary (see Moving on a Gripper Strip Frame, page 41).

1 Border stitch (6 stitches per inch) with the medium blue yarn to trace the scallop line. Use the fill stitch (4 stitches per inch) to section and fill inside the scallop, stopping as you reach the florals.

2 Using pale blue yarn, outline the scalloped shapes with one row of border stitch. Punch two rows of border stitch around the perimeter of the rug. Fill the background area with fill stitch. *fig. A*

3 Move on to the floral elements within the frame. Trace the flowers in off-white border stitch, then fill. Outline the stems and leaves in dark blue, then fill. Outline the florals with medium blue border stitch, then fill in all the remaining space in the frame. *fig. B*

4 Carefully pull one end of the monks cloth up and off the grippers to loosen the overall tension, then roll it toward the punched part of the project and off the frame. Restretch on the frame with the new area centered. *fig. C*

TIP A frame cover can be very helpful in keeping the rug in place on a gripper strip frame. Beyond protecting your arms, it can also help keep large rugs from pulling away from the gripper needles.

5 Repeat Steps 1–4 to punch the rug. Always include two rows of border stitches along the outer perimeter of the rug. Steam press as you go. *figs. D-G*

STEAM PRESS AS YOU GO
Since this is a larger project, steam press as you go. Large rugs often curl as they are punched, so heat and steam will be your friends in relaxing the loops and keeping things manageable. Remove the rug from the frame. Press the rug with a damp towel and hot iron to relax the loops, making the rug less unruly and easier to work with as it grows. See Blocking (page 43) for more details. Once it is pressed and easier to handle, lay the piece back over the frame and tighten the monks cloth.

FINISHING

1 Carefully remove the project from the frame. If you have not done so already, push all yarn tails through the backing with a narrow pair of scissors, or the punch needle. Punch in any remaining gaps. Flip the piece over and cut the tails flush to the loop pile.

2 Tidy the loops by pushing them into place with the scissors or punch needle. Take your time to define the shapes (see Tidying Loops, page 42).

3 On a heatproof surface, lay a damp towel over the loop side of the rug. Press the rug with the appropriate heat setting on the iron. If necessary, use this process to correct any shaping issues, pressing out any unwanted irregularities with steam and heat (see Blocking, page 43). Let dry in place.

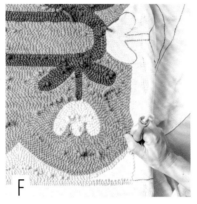

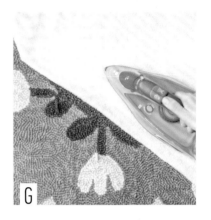

Stitch spacing will often change through the process on a larger rug, sometimes making an irregular overall shape. If needed, pin down the shape while blocking thoroughly to correct the shape and allow it to dry completely (this can take 1–2 days). If the shape is still not right, stitch additional border stitches around the perimeter of the rug to correct any unevenness, and press again.

TIP Wool yarn has a unique set of properties: The exterior of the fiber is hydrophobic and repels water, while the core is hydroscopic and holds on to water. Once water has penetrated the core of the wool fibers, it can take a long time for them to dry. Keep this in mind during the blocking process—you'll want the fibers wet enough to reshape, and to let them *fully dry* before moving them.

4 Once you're happy with the overall shape, trim the monks cloth, leaving a 3″ perimeter on all sides of the rug.

5 Hem the monks cloth to the stitch side of the rug (see Hemming, page 44) with heavy-duty thread. If desired, shave the rug with a fabric shaver or lint roller for a smooth finish. *fig. H*

woven plaid chair pad

FINISHED SIZE: 13″ × 14″–16″ (custom sizing recommended)

A ¼″ loop pile is an excellent all-purpose pile height! It's practical, easy to keep clean, and still feels like a treat to sit, lie, or walk on. Rugs, pillows, seat cushions—it works for them all! This pattern is adaptable to many different seat sizes, and I recommend that you make it a custom size for your home. Simply repeat the warp and weft woven design elements to suit the shape you're working with. Wouldn't it be lovely over a long wooden bench?

I've made mine for an antique wooden chair with a seat measuring 16″ at the back, tapering out to 18″ at the front, with a length of 15″. So my chair pad measures 14″ at the back, tapering out to 16″ at the front, and is 13″ in length. To determine the amount of backing and yarn you need for your custom-size chair pad, see Calculating Yarn and Backing Amounts (page 67).

BACKING AND YARN

Monks cloth (12–14 holes per inch) with edges finished, sized to your own chair or bench (23″ × 26″)

12½ oz. bulky weight wool rug yarn in off-white

2 oz. bulky weight wool rug yarn in neon yellow

2 oz. bulky weight wool rug yarn in pink

1 oz. bulky weight wool rug yarn in green

1 oz. bulky weight wool rug yarn in medium blue

1 oz. bulky weight wool rug yarn in dark blue

1 oz. bulky weight wool rug yarn in red

Additional long scrap yarn strands for ties (optional)

TOOLS

Gripper strip frame and cover

Oxford Punch Needle, regular size 10

Black permanent marker

Scissors

Iron and towel

Paper

Masking tape

Hand-sewing needle and all-purpose thread

Fabric shaver or lint roller (optional)

Woven Plaid pattern (see Projects, page 68)

note

Remember, you can always use any of the punch needle or frame variations we reviewed in Tools and Materials (page 14)! Just make sure you're using a punch needle that punches 1/4″ loops with bulky yarn. For more detailed information about each step, see Setting Up (page 30) and Punch Needle Rug Hooking Basics (page 34).

SETTING UP

1 Finish the edges of the backing (see Preparing the Backing, page 30). Create a custom paper pattern by tracing the seat of your chair. Subtract 2″ to all sides of the seat so the cushion will be smaller than the chair. Then transfer the Woven Plaid pattern to your custom-size paper (see Transferring the Pattern, page 30). If you prefer, freehand the design onto the backing for your own personal touch. Transfer the pattern to the backing.

2 Set the backing onto the frame with the design set in the middle. Tighten all sides of the backing onto the frame until the pattern is taut, but do not distort the design. Slip the cover over the frame.

TIP If you prefer a clean, geometric finish, use a ruler to draw the pattern. Then use a consistent number of stitch rows in each stripe, and between stripes.

PUNCHING

1 Trace the first vertical stripe of color in neon yellow with a border stitch (6 stitches per inch). Where it meets the perimeters of the chair pad, stitch two rows of border stitches. Stop punching when another stripe will intersect over top of the line. Fill the stripe with a fill stitch (4 stitches per inch).

2 Repeat Step 1 to stitch vertical and horizontal stripes in pink, green, medium blue, dark blue, neon yellow, and red, as shown. Take your time at the intersections where colors meet, making sure the lines don't get skewed where the colors butt against one another. Feel free to remove yarn and try again if needed. *fig. A*

3 Outline all the stripes in off-white border stitches. Add two rows of border stitches along the perimeter of the chair pad. Fill with fill stitch. *fig. B*

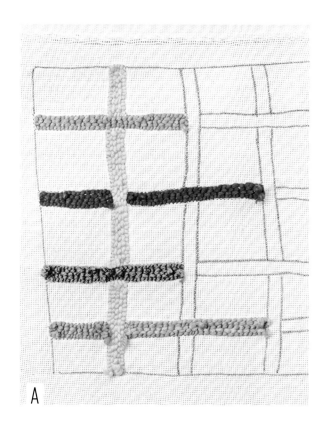

A

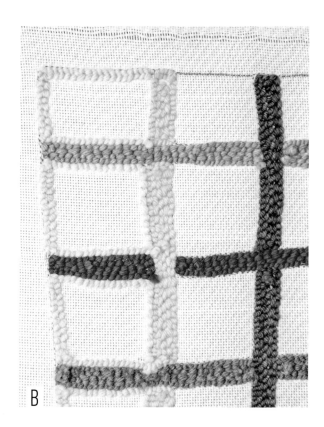

B

4 If necessary, move the piece on the frame (see Moving on a Gripper Strip Frame, page 41), and repeat Steps 1–3 to fill in all the stripes and background. *figs. C-D*

FINISHING

1 Carefully remove the project from the frame. If you have not done so already, push all yarn tails through the backing with a narrow pair of scissors, or the punch needle. Punch in any remaining gaps. Flip the piece over and cut the tails flush to the loop pile.

2 Tidy the loops by pushing them into place with the scissors or punch needle. Take your time to define the crisp lines (see Tidying Loops, page 42).

3 On a heatproof surface, lay a damp towel over the loop side of the rug. Press the rug with the appropriate heat setting on the iron. If necessary, use this process to correct any shaping issues, pressing out any unwanted irregularities with steam and heat (see Blocking, page 43). Let dry in place.

4 Trim the monks cloth, leaving a 3″ perimeter on all sides of the rug.

5 Hem the monks cloth to the stitch side of the rug (see Hemming, page 44) with the all-purpose thread. If desired, shave the rug with a fabric shaver or lint roller for a smooth finish.

OPTIONAL: CHAIR TIES

There are many ways to secure your chair pad in place if you'd like to. This method works for chairs with both spindles or back posts. Gather 3 strands of yarn 21″ long. Tie the yarns together at one end with a knot, and then braid it. Tie a knot at the bottom to secure the braid. Repeat to make two braids. Stitch the center of one braid to the back corner of the cushion using the needle and thread. Repeat with the other braid and corner. *fig. E*

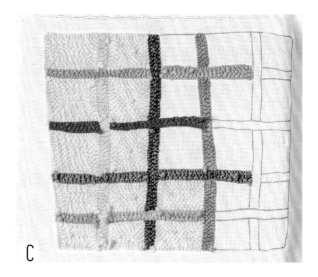

C

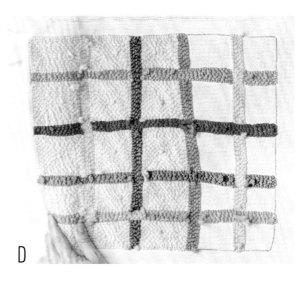

D

E

vintage carousel rug

FINISHED SIZE: 23″ × 31″

In older rug designs, it is common to come across unconventional color combinations because when one color ran out, the artist used whatever they had to continue punching. Occasionally, I intentionally do the same as a fun way to add a bit of character. If you take a closer look, you'll notice that I've substituted a different shade of green in one of the flower leaves.

This is entirely optional when you make this project, but it also serves as a reminder that you're free to use the colors you have available. Even if the colors don't match perfectly, the results can turn out surprisingly lovely! If, in the end, you're not satisfied with how it looks, simply pull out the yarn and try something different. This craft allows for experimentation without much risk of damaging your final piece.

BACKING AND YARN

Monks cloth (12–14 holes per inch) with edges finished: 29½″ × 36″

23½ oz. bulky weight wool rug yarn in light cream

15 oz. bulky weight wool rug yarn in gold

10½ oz. bulky weight wool rug yarn in charcoal

3 oz. bulky weight wool rug yarn in green

TOOLS

Gripper strip frame and cover

Oxford Punch Needle, regular size 10

Black permanent marker

Scissors

Iron and towel

Hand-sewing needle and heavy-duty thread (upholstery or button and craft)

Sewing pins

Paper

Masking tape

Fabric shaver or lint roller (optional)

Vintage Carousel pattern (see Projects, page 68)

note

Remember, you can always use any of the punch needle or frame variations we reviewed in Tools and Materials (page 14)! Just make sure you're using a punch needle that punches 1/4″ loops with bulky yarn. For this project, I recommend a gripper strip frame or similar so that tension can be adjusted while working. For more detailed information about each step, see Setting Up (page 30) and Punch Needle Rug Hooking Basics (page 34).

SETTING UP

1 Finish the edges of the backing (see Preparing the Backing, page 30). Transfer the pattern to the backing (see Transferring the Pattern, page 30). If you prefer, freehand the design onto the backing for your own personal touch.

2 Set the backing onto the frame with the lower left part of the design in the middle. Tighten all sides of the backing onto the frame until the pattern is taut, but do not distort the design. Slip the cover over the frame.

PUNCHING

1 With charcoal, border stitch (6 stitches per inch) to outline the horse's mane, tail, and legs. Fill them with a charcoal fill stitch (4 stitches per inch). Still using charcoal, outline the repeating scallop elements, and fill them with the fill stitch. *fig. A*

2 In gold, stitch two rows of border stitches around the outer perimeter of the rug, and one row of border stitching against the flat side of the scallops. If necessary, add a row of fill stitch to finish the border. Border stitch and fill the body of the horse and the hooves. In green, border stitch and fill the stem. *fig. B*

3 Using the light cream, border stitch around the horse's body and hooves, the scallops, and the stem. Fill in the whole background with the fill stitch. Be mindful of overpacking in densely stitched areas like between the horses back legs and in between scallops.

4 Reposition the piece on the frame to center the upper left section of the rug (see Moving on a Gripper Strip Frame, page 41). Outline and fill the charcoal scallops. Outline and fill the center of the flower in charcoal. Outline and fill the flower petals in gold. Outline all of the interior shapes with light cream. Fill. Finally, punch two rows of gold border stitching along the outer perimeter, and one along the flat side of the scallops. Fill if necessary. *fig. C*

5 Reposition the rug on the frame again, centering the horses. Punch the eyes in charcoal using three tight border stitches. Punch a tight circle of border stitches in gold around the eyes (I used seven stitches). Border stitch and fill the manes in charcoal. *fig. D*

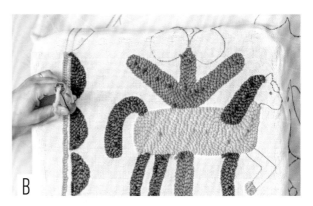

6 Continue making your way around the rug, moving it as you finish each section. Block the rug if necessary so that the rug lies cooperatively alongside your frame as you work. Stitch the horse bodies, heads, and hooves in gold. Stitch the horse legs, manes, and tails in charcoal. Continue the border and scallops in gold and charcoal. Stitch the flowers and stems in charcoal, gold, and green. Outline and fill all background spaces with light cream. *figs. E-G*

FINISHING

1 Carefully remove the project from the frame. If you have not done so already, push all yarn tails through the backing with a narrow pair of scissors, or the punch needle. Punch in any remaining gaps. Flip the piece over and cut the tails flush to the loop pile.

2 Tidy the loops by pushing them into place with the scissors or punch needle. Take your time to define the shapes, especially around the eyes (see Tidying Loops, page 42).

3 On a heatproof surface, lay a damp towel over the loop side of the rug. Press the rug with the appropriate heat setting on the iron. If necessary, use this process to correct any shaping issues, pressing out any unwanted irregularities with steam and heat (see Blocking, page 43). Let dry in place.

4 Trim the monks cloth to have a 3″ perimeter on all sides of the rug.

5 Hem the monks cloth to the stitch side of the rug (see Hemming, page 44) with the upholstery or heavy-duty thread. If desired, shave the rug with a fabric shaver or lint roller for a smooth finish.

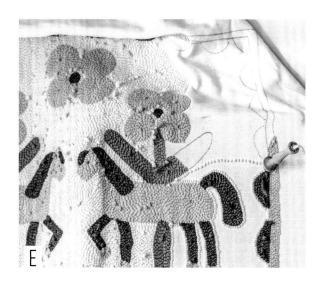

E

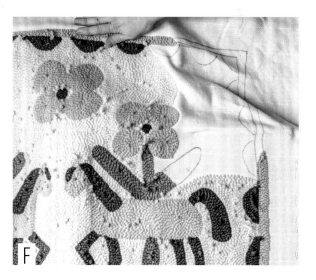

F

G

spring snake bolster pillow

FINISHED SIZE: 31″ × 6¼″

This snake is as friendly as they come! One of the great things about stuffing a pillow punched with rug wool is the sturdiness of the overall pillow form, which allows for a variety of stuffing options. For example, I've used worn-out T-shirts and my daughter's old clothing to stuff mine. It's a useful way to recycle or keep old textiles that are too sentimental to part with. This type of stuffing material wouldn't be comfortable for a standard fabric pillow, but it works perfectly under the dense pile of the rug yarn. If you want to make this snake even more unique, consider stitching it with two heads!

BACKING AND YARN

Monks cloth (12–14 holes per inch) with edges finished: 41″ × 42¼″

3 oz. bulky weight wool rug yarn in brick red

½ oz. bulky weight wool rug yarn in charcoal

17 oz. bulky weight wool rug yarn in yellow

23¾ oz. bulky weight wool rug yarn in off-white

8½″ × 8½″ piece of dense card stock or cardboard

Materials for stuffing (scraps, pillow insert, stuffing, or old clothing)

TOOLS

Gripper strip frame and cover

Oxford Punch Needle, regular size 10

Black permanent marker

Scissors

Iron and towel

Hand-sewing needle and heavy-duty thread (upholstery or button and craft)

All-purpose thread in red

Tapestry/yarn needle

Sewing pins

Paper

Masking tape

Fabric shaver or lint roller (optional)

Spring Snake pattern (see Projects, page 68)

note

Remember, you can always use any of the punch needle or frame variations we reviewed in Tools and Materials (page 14)! Just make sure you're using a punch needle that punches 1/4″ loops with bulky yarn. For this project, I recommend a gripper strip frame or similar so that tension can be adjusted while working. For more detailed information about each step, see Setting Up (page 30) and Punch Needle Rug Hooking Basics (page 34).

SETTING UP

1 Finish the edges of the backing (see Preparing the Backing, page 30). Transfer the pattern to the backing (see Transferring the Pattern, page 30). If you prefer, freehand the stripes and eyes onto the backing for your own personal touch.

note

It's a good idea to keep all of the pattern elements together on one piece of monks cloth (with a minimum of 6″ of seam allowance between each shape) unless you have a small frame that can accommodate the small circular ends individually on small pieces of monks cloth.

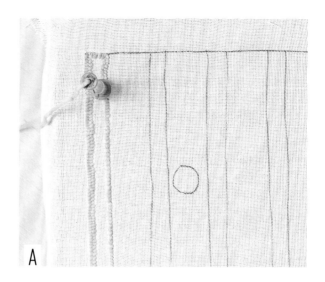

A

2 Set the backing onto the frame with the upper left side of the pattern set in the middle. Tighten all sides of the backing onto the frame until the pattern is taut, but do not distort the design. Slip the cover over the frame.

PUNCHING

1 Using a border stitch (6 stitches per inch), punch two rows of yellow yarn around the outside perimeter of the first stripe. Continue with one row of border stitches to outline the first stripe. Fill in with a fill stitch (4 stitches per inch). *fig. A*

TIP I've staggered the length at which I end my stripes so that when I continue them after moving the piece on the frame, the joints don't draw attention to one area/line. Staggering the stop/start areas gives a more natural and even loop pile.

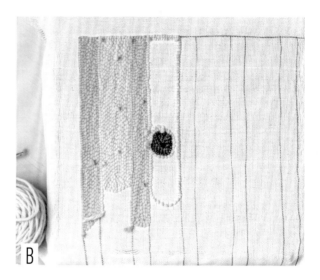

B

2 Outline the second stripe in off-white using the border stitch, with two rows of border stitches along the upper perimeter of the pattern. Fill the second stripe with the fill stitch.

3 In charcoal, outline and fill the eye. Outline the eye in off-white and continue with the stripes, repeating Steps 1 and 2 to punch the stripes in alternating colors. Move the project on the frame as necessary (see Moving on a Gripper Strip Frame, page 41) until you've punched the entire upper half of the project. *figs. B-C*

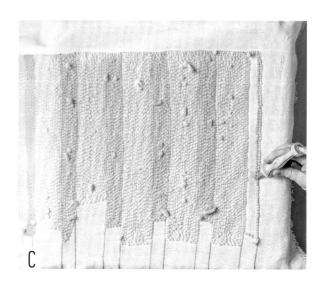

C

4 Reposition the rug on the frame to access the lower half of the stripes, and repeat Steps 1–3 connecting to the upper stripe stitches. Be mindful not to cluster the tails. Continue punching until all the stripes have been outlined and filled. *fig. D*

5 Outline and fill the two pillow ends, in yellow yarn. If you only have a large frame, punch these circles before cutting away any monks cloth. Or stitch them separately on a smaller frame. This is an easy shape to start from the outside and spiral toward the center. *fig. E*

FINISHING

1 Carefully remove the project from the frame. If you have not done so already, push all yarn tails through the backing with a narrow pair of scissors, or a punch needle. Punch in any remaining gaps. Flip the piece over and cut the tails flush to the loop pile.

2 Tidy the loops by pushing them into place with the scissors or punch needle. Take your time to define the shapes if you want crisp stripes (see Tidying Loops, page 42).

3 On a heatproof surface, lay a damp towel over the loop side of the pattern pieces. Press them with the appropriate heat setting on the iron. If necessary, use this process to correct any shaping issues, pressing out any unwanted irregularities with steam and heat (see Blocking, page 43). Let dry in place.

CONSTRUCTION

1 Cut a 3″ seam allowance around all three forms.

2 With pile sides folded together lengthwise and stripes matched together, pin the two sides together. Loosely stitch the two sides of monks cloth together with a backstitch (page 51). The length of the backstitch can be 1″ or larger for speed, as this is just a basting stitch line meant to hold the piece together while you turn it right side out. *fig. F*

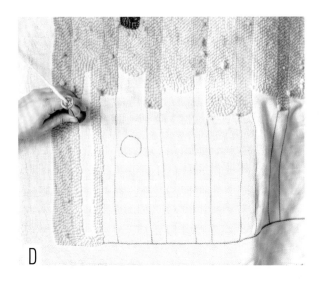

D

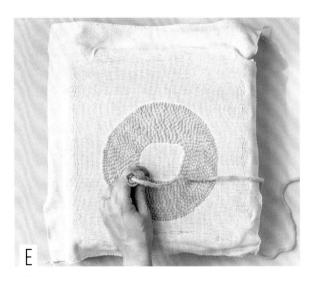

E

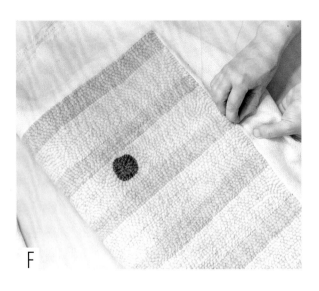

F

3 Turn the pillow pile side out by gently folding one edge in, and with your other hand, guiding that same edge toward the other end of the pillow and out. *fig. G*

4 Hand stitch the full length of the pillow body using a ladder stitch (page 50). Stitch up to the very edge of both sides of the loops and pull them together to conceal any visible monks cloth. Anchor the thread (see Anchoring Thread, page 48) every so often to minimize the strain on the line of stitching. *fig. H*

5 Position one pillow round at one end of the snake, pile side out, and with seam allowance tucked into the pillow form. Pin if needed. Sew the round to the body of the pillow using the ladder stitch, again stitching close to the edge of both sides of loop lines. Pull the stitch line taut to connect the two sides and conceal any visible monks cloth. *fig. I*

6 Stuff the pillow form with your choice of stuffing. If you're using used clothing, avoid items with hard edges, zippers, or buttons. *fig. J*

7 Close the pillow form with the second yellow round, repeating Step 5.

G

H

I

J

8 Using the 8½″ × 8½″ piece of cardboard or card stock, wrap brick-red yarn around the form 10 times. Slide the yarn off, gather it at the center, and tie a long piece of brick-red yarn tightly around it (keeping a long tail for sewing the following steps). *figs. K-L*

Fold the yarn loops in half, and with another separate piece of matching yarn, gather and tie the bundle of yarn securely, 1½″ from the fold, creating a small round bundle. Wrap the attached length of yarn around the bundle tightly (3–4 times) to conceal the knot. Thread the tail of yarn into a yarn needle, and weave it back into the knotted area to secure it. *fig. M*

9 Thread the tail of the red all-purpose sewing thread into the yarn needle, and sew the tongue (tassel) to the center of the yellow round end (by the eyes), securing the tassel to the snake. Make sure it's pulled taut to secure it and to conceal your thread within the tassel. *fig. N*

10 If desired, shave the rug with a fabric shaver or lint roller for a smooth finish.

K

L

M

N

changing weather clutch

FINISHED SIZE: 14″ × 11″

I'm always on the lookout for ways to organize my favorite craft supplies. This soft and floppy clutch is the perfect place for corralling punch needles, rug hooks, patterns, and knitting needles … or any manner of lovely things that are special to you. It keeps them together and highlights the joy they bring, because once you open the clutch, sunny days appear! If you'd like to take this project further, line the interior in a matching fabric before moving on to folding and whipstitching, or add a button closure on the flap!

BACKING AND YARN

Monks cloth (12–14 holes per inch) with edges finished: 24″ × 35″

20 oz. bulky weight wool rug yarn in sky blue

4½ oz. bulky weight wool rug yarn off-white

1½ oz. bulky weight wool rug yarn in orange-red

1½ oz. bulky weight wool rug yarn in yellow

1 oz. bulky weight wool rug yarn in charcoal

TOOLS

Gripper strip frame and cover

Oxford Punch Needle, regular size 10

Black permanent marker

Scissors

Iron and towel

Hand-sewing needle and heavy-duty thread (upholstery or button and craft thread)

Tapestry/yarn needle

Paper

Masking tape

Fabric shaver or lint roller (optional)

Changing Weather pattern (see Projects, page 68)

note

Remember, you can always use any of the punch needle or frame variations we reviewed in Tools and Materials (page 14)! Just make sure you're using a punch needle that punches 1/4″ loops with bulky yarn. For this project, I recommend a gripper strip frame or similar so that tension can be adjusted while working. For more detailed information about each step, see Setting Up (page 30) and Punch Needle Rug Hooking Basics (page 34).

SETTING UP

1 Finish the edges of the backing (see Preparing the Backing, page 30). Transfer the pattern to the backing (see Transferring the Pattern, page 30). If you prefer, freehand the design onto the backing for your own personal touch. Take note of the fold lines and mark them on both the front and the back (pile and stitch side) of the monks cloth for reference during construction. Once you mark them on the stitch side, they should be visible enough to trace on the pile side.

2 Set the backing onto the frame with the top left end of the clutch design set in the middle. Tighten all sides of the backing onto the frame until the pattern is taut, but do not distort the design. Slip the cover over the frame.

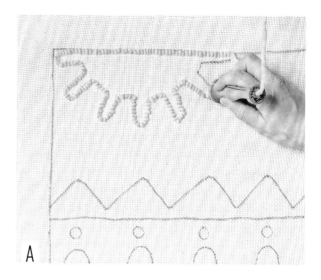

A

PUNCHING

1 Outline the sun in yellow using border stitches (6 stitches per inch) with two rows of border stitching on the top perimeter of the clutch. Fill the sun with fill stitch (4 stitches per inch). *fig. A*

2 In orange-red, outline the neighborhood rooflines using border stitch, and fill with fill stitch. Continue outlining and filling the windows and doors in charcoal. *fig. B*

TIP I started by stitching the windows in blue and the doorways in charcoal, but eventually decided I wanted them to be the same color. So I removed the blue windows and restitched them in charcoal. If you'd prefer to use blue for the windows, replace the 1 oz. of charcoal yarn with sky blue yarn. Choose whatever colors suit you, and remember that you can always switch things up!

3 Border stitch under the roofline, around the doors and windows, and the base of the houses in off-white yarn. Punch two rows at the exterior of the pattern. Fill the houses. *fig. C*

note

At the base of the houses (where the fold lines are marked), punch a little more densely than the standard fill stitch so that the backing doesn't show when the project is folded.

B

C

4 In sky blue, punch two rows of border stitches around the outer perimeter of the clutch. Outline the design elements. Section off areas and fill in the background with the fill stitch. Move the project on the frame to finish the house and background (see Moving on a Gripper Strip Frame, page 41). *figs. D-E*

5 Move the project on the frame to center the second half. Outline and fill the clouds in off-white. Outline the clouds and perimeter in sky blue, using two rows of border stitches on the outside edges. *fig. F*

6 Fill the rest of the piece in sky blue. Move the piece as necessary to punch any unfinished areas.

FINISHING AND CONSTRUCTION

1 Carefully remove the project from the frame. If you have not done so already, push all yarn tails through the backing with a narrow pair of scissors, or the punch needle. Punch in any remaining gaps. Flip the piece over and cut the tails flush to the loop pile.

2 Tidy the loops by pushing them into place with the scissors or punch needle. Take your time to define the shapes.

3 On a heatproof surface, lay a damp towel over the loop side of the rug. Press the rug with the appropriate heat setting on the iron. If necessary, use this process to correct any shaping issues, pressing out any unwanted irregularities with steam and heat (see Blocking, page 43). Let dry in place.

4 Trim the monks cloth to a perimeter of 3″ around the project. Hem the perimeter (see Hemming, page 44). Press the fold again to set the hem. *fig. G*

D

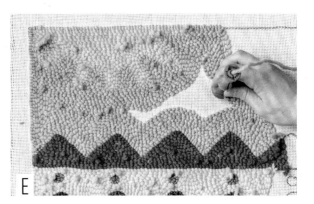

E

F

G

5 With the loop side facing down, fold the clutch at the fold line. *fig. H*

6 Starting with off-white at the bottom of the folded edge, connect the two sides of the clutch by whipstitching (page 48) the yarn to close the gap. The whipstitching should extend to the yarn loops on both sides, and leave no monks cloth visible. Continue to the orange-red roofline and cut a 1½″ tail. *fig. I*

7 Begin whipstitching again, this time with orange-red yarn. Align and conceal the off-white tail with the orange-red whipstitches as you conceal the monks cloth. Whipstitch until you reach the blue skyline, and cut a 1 ½″ tail. Repeat the process with the sky-blue yarn, concealing the orange-red tail. *figs. J-K*

H

I

J

K

8 After you reach the top of the folded edge, continue whipstitching in sky blue, this time without connecting two sides. The stitches should extend about ¼″ into the hemmed monks cloth, neatly wrapping the edge for a polished finish. Keep consistent tension to avoid pulling the stitches too tight and warping the clutch. *fig. L*

9 Continue whipstitching to the top of the piece, around the perimeter of the top flap, and back down. Then join the other side of the clutch, repeating Steps 11 and 12 (switching colors to match the yarn and burying tails). Cut a 2½″ tail and weave it through the center of the whipstitching to secure it. *fig. M*

10 If desired, shave the clutch with a fabric shaver or lint roller for a smooth finish.

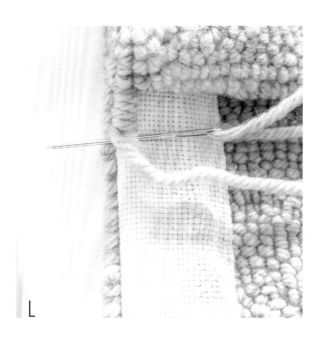

L

M

RESOURCES

DYES

Majic Carpet Dyes: **wandaworks.ca**

PRO Chemical & Dye: **prochemicalanddye.net**

Jacquard Products: **jacquardproducts.com**

Dharma Trading: **dharmatrading.com**

BACKING, TOOLS, AND FRAMES

Ribbon Candy Hooking: **ribboncandyhooking.com**

Kevin LeMoine: **punchneedlerughooking.ca**

Punch Needle World: **punchneedleworld.com**

The Oxford Company: **amyoxford.com**

Deanne Fitzpatrick Studio: **hookingrugs.com**

Dorr Mill Store: **dorrmillstore.com**

Punch Needle World: **punchneedleworld.com**

The Woolery: **woolery.com**

Whole Punching: **wholepunching.co.uk**

WOOL RUG YARNS

Briggs & Little Woolen Mills Ltd.: **briggsandlittle.com**

Punch Needle World: **punchneedleworld.com**

Seal Harbor Rug Company: **sealharborrug.com**

Violet Jane: **amyoxford.com/pages/violet-jane-yarn**

Story Teller Wool: **shopstorytellerwool.com**

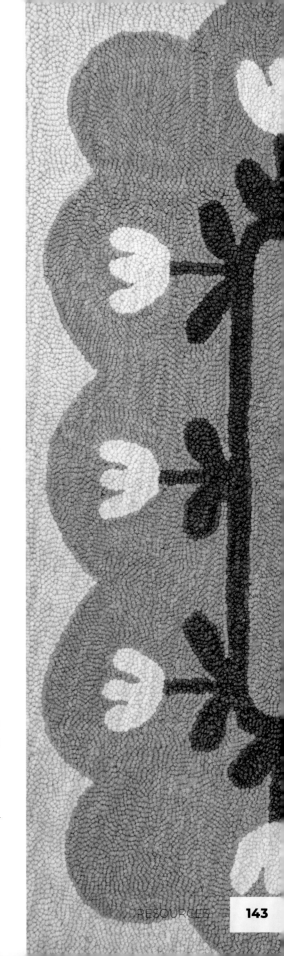

SOURCES

Edward M. Langille, The Story of Lillian Burke, Big Bras d'Or, NS: Boularderie Island Press, 2019.

Mildred Cole Péladeau, Rug Hooking in Maine, 1838 -1940. Atglen, PA: Schiffer Publishing 2008.

Amy Oxford, Punch Needle Rug Hooking, Your Complete Resource to Learn and Love the Craft Atglen, PA: Schiffer Publishing, 2020.

Anselme Chiasson and Annie-Rose Deveau, The History of Chéticamp Hooked Rugs and their Artisans. A Project of La Société Saint- Pierre, Translated by Marcel LeBlanc. Yarmouth, NS: Lescarbot Publications, 1988.

Clasper-Torch, Micah. The History of Punch Needle. Sister- Mag. NO 61, May 2021 Carry-On Publishing. sister-mag.com/en/magazine/sistermag-no-61-may-2021/the-history-of-punch-needle/#:~:text=Throughout%20 the%201800s%2C%20rug%20hooking,to%20the%20traditional%20 rug%20hook

Ryan, Nanette and Doreen Wright, Garretts and the Bluenose Rugs of Nova Scotia, Mahone, Bay, NS: reprinted by Spruce Top Rug Hooking Studio, 1995

The Teachers Branch, Rug hooking guild of Nova Scotia, The Garrett Bluenose Patterns, Celebrating Nova Scotia's Rug Hooking Heritage, Halifax, NS: Nimbus Publishing Limited, 2022.

Canadian Museum of Civilization: historymuseum.ca/cmc/exhibitions/ arts/rugs/rugs01e.html

Helaine Fendelman and Joe Rosson, Treasures: Hooked rug's value is in sentiment, May, 2011 Seattle Times seattletimes.com/life/lifestyle/ treasures-hooked-rugs-value-is-in-sentiment

American artist Lillian Burke with Cheticamp hooked rug and the women who made it; Nancy Korber, Librarian/Archivist, Fairchild Tropical Botanic Garden from the collection of photographer Dr. David Fairchild; Used under Creative Commons Attribution-ShareAlike 3.0 Unported license, commons.wikimedia.org/wiki/File:American_artist_Lillian_Burke_with_ Cheticamp_hooked_rug_and_the_women_who_made_it.tif#mw-jump-to-license

ABOUT THE AUTHOR

Crystal Ross is a Canadian artist and graduate of NSCAD U, a place where she spent much of her time in various textile departments. Drawing inspiration from her familial roots, Crystal turned to crafting hand-hooked rugs and now uses a blend of traditional hooks and punch needles in her work. Her maternal grandparents, both expert rug hookers from Chéticamp, Nova Scotia (a place steeped in rug hooking history), dedicated much of their lives to the art form: producing beautiful mats, teaching the craft, and promoting its unique local history.

Crystal's own work is a playful take on the tradition, combining her love of Nova Scotian folk art and modern forms. Her pieces are collected throughout Canada and the United States, and she has been featured in many design publications including *Label* magazine, *Remodelista*, and *Chatelaine* magazine.

Based in Dartmouth, Nova Scotia, Crystal works from her home studio, where she shares the creative space with her family and a lively pair of animals.

Visit Crystal online and follow on social media!

WEBSITE: crystalrugs.ca

INSTAGRAM: @crystalrugs